A Theory of Accumulation and Secular Stagnation

DOI: 10.1057/9781137562210.0001

Other Palgrave Pivot titles

Indranarain Ramlall: **Central Bank Ratings: A New Methodology for Global Excellence**

Stephen Paul Miller: **The New Deal as a Triumph of Social Work: Frances Perkins and the Confluence of Early Twentieth Century Social Work with Mid-Twentieth Century Politics and Government**

Nicholas Pamment: **Community Reparation for Young Offenders: Perceptions, Policy and Practice**

David F. Tennant and Marlon R. Tracey: **Sovereign Debt and Credit Rating Bias**

Jefferson Walker: **King Returns to Washington: Explorations of Memory, Rhetoric, and Politics in the Martin Luther King, Jr. National Memorial**

Giovanni Barone Adesi and Nicola Carcano: **Modern Multi-Factor Analysis of Bond Portfolios: Critical Implications for Hedging and Investing**

Rilka Dragneva and Kataryna Wolczuk: **Ukraine between the EU and Russia: The Integration Challenge**

Viola Fabbrini, Massimo Guidolin and Manuela Pedio: **The Transmission Channels of Financial Shocks to Stock, Bond, and Asset-Backed Markets: An Empirical Analysis**

Timothy Wood: **Detainee Abuse During Op TELIC: 'A Few Rotten Apples'?**

Lars Klüver, Rasmus Øjvind Nielsen and Marie Louise Jørgensen (editors): **Policy-Oriented Technology Assessment Across Europe: Expanding Capacities**

Rebecca E. Lyons and Samantha J. Rayner (editors): **The Academic Book of the Future**

Ben Clements: **Surveying Christian Beliefs and Religious Debates in Post-War Britain**

Robert A. Stebbins: **Leisure and the Motive to Volunteer: Theories of Serious, Casual, and Project-Based Leisure**

Dietrich Orlow: **Socialist Reformers and the Collapse of the German Democratic Republic**

Gwendolyn Audrey Foster: **Disruptive Feminisms: Raced, Gendered, and Classed Bodies in Film**

Catherine A. Lugg: **US Public Schools and the Politics of Queer Erasure**

Olli Pyyhtinen: **More-than-Human Sociology: A New Sociological Imagination**

Jane Hemsley-Brown and Izhar Oplatka: **Higher Education Consumer Choice**

Arthur Asa Berger: **Gizmos or: The Electronic Imperative: How Digital Devices have Transformed American Character and Culture**

Antoine Vauchez: **Democratizing Europe**

DOI: 10.1057/9781137562210.0001

palgrave▸pivot

A Theory of Accumulation and Secular Stagnation: A Malthusian Approach to Understanding a Contemporary Malaise

Daniel Aronoff

President, Landon Companies, USA

palgrave macmillan

DOI: 10.1057/9781137562210.0001

A THEORY OF ACCUMULATION AND SECULAR STAGNATION

First published 2016 by
PALGRAVE MACMILLAN

Palgrave Macmillan in the UK is an imprint of Macmillan Publishers Limited, registered in England, company number 785998, of Houndmills, Basingstoke, Hampshire, RG21 6XS.

Palgrave Macmillan in the US is a division of Nature America, Inc., One New York Plaza, Suite 4500 New York, NY 10004-1562.

Palgrave Macmillan is the global academic imprint of the above companies and has companies and representatives throughout the world.

Hardback ISBN: 978-1-137-56220-3
E-PUB ISBN: 978-1-137-56222-7
E-PDF ISBN: 978-1-137-56221-0
DOI: 10.1057/9781137562210

Distribution in the UK, Europe and the rest of the world is by Palgrave Macmillan®, a division of Macmillan Publishers Limited, registered in England, company number 785998, of Houndmills, Basingstoke, Hampshire RG21 6XS.

Library of Congress Cataloging-in-Publication Data is available from the Library of Congress

A catalog record for this book is available from the Library of Congress

A catalogue record for the book is available from the British Library

This book is dedicated to the memory of my father, Arnold Aronoff, with whom I shared the privilege of a lifelong discussion of politics, history and economics, and to my son Joseph Aronoff, with whom I now share the privilege of continuing the discussion

DOI: 10.1057/9781137562210.0001

Contents

List of Illustrations vii

Introduction 1

Part I The Malthus–Ricardo Debate

1 The Malthus–Ricardo Debate on General Glut and Secular Stagnation 10

2 Say's Principle and the Possibility of Deficient Demand 44

Part II Accumulation and Secular Stagnation in the Contemporary United States

3 The Theory of Accumulation and Secular Stagnation 67

4 Accumulation and Secular Stagnation in the United States after the Turn of the Millennium 88

Some Concluding Thoughts 124

Name Index 128

Subject Index 130

DOI: 10.1057/9781137562210.0001

List of Illustrations

Figures

1.1 The relation between investment and output over time in Adam Smith's model 13

1.2 The relation between income and consumption for different social classes in Malthus's model 18

1.3 The relation between income and expenditure assuming constant investment in Malthus's model 19

1.4 The movement of output and prices in Malthus's short-term cycle 24

2.1 The relation of output, employment, real wages, and profit for the economy described by Malthus and Ricardo 54

3.1 The federal funds rate and the ten-year treasury yield (2004–2007) 71

4.1 The China/US FX rate (1990–2008) and bi-lateral trade balance (1999–2014) 90

4.2 The income share and earnings of top 1% and 0.1% of earners in the US (1980–2012) 101

4.3 US real median household income and labor force participation (1984–2012) 107

4.4 Statistical analysis of relation of change in federal funds rate and ten-year treasury yield (1985–2005) 115

Table

2.1 Aggregate budget matrix for an economy 48

DOI: 10.1057/9781137562210.0002

palgrave▸pivot

www.palgrave.com/pivot

Introduction

Abstract: *This book explores and extends Thomas Malthus's idea that if an economically significant group saves a large portion of income it plans never to spend, it will cause a deficiency in demand that prevents a market economy from operating at full employment on a sustainable basis—Accumulation is the portion of saving that is intended never to be spent. Accumulation causes secular stagnation—a condition of low growth and underemployment of resources and it provides fertile ground for periodic, but unsustainable, booms. Accumulation places bounds on possible outcomes; actual outcomes depend upon the institutional structure of the economy and the expectations of its participants. Malthus's idea is coherent—contrary to the conventional wisdom—and it can be used to understand the cause of the low growth and tepid employment, periodically punctuated by booms, that has plagued the US economy since the turn of the millennium. It is explained that offshore mercantilists—principally China—and top income earners has been driving Accumulation in the US economy in recent decades.*

Aronoff, Daniel. *A Theory of Accumulation and Secular Stagnation: A Malthusian Approach to Understanding a Contemporary Malaise*. New York: Palgrave Macmillan, 2016. DOI: 10.1057/9781137562210.0003.

1 Concept of this book

This book is about an idea in economics. Its conceit is that the idea has deep subterranean historical roots and that it can explain an important contemporary economic phenomenon. The idea may appear to be novel; and it is in some respects, while in others it is not. The idea can be thought of using the metaphor of a golden key that promises to unlock the door of an enigmatic safe. This key was fashioned a long time ago, by a man named Thomas Robert Malthus (1766–1834). At the time—nearly 200 years ago—there was a rival safecracker named David Ricardo (1772–1823), who learned his craft from a master safecracker ("the" master safecracker) named Adam Smith (1723–1790) (Malthus also learned from Smith, but he was considered a bastard child). Ricardo's key was thought to be more promising than Malthus key, and so over time economists paid little attention to Malthus's key. They forgot about it so completely that they forgot it ever existed.

Around a hundred years later another crackerjack safecracker named Keynes appeared on the scene and he did some rummaging around with a guide named Sraffa[1] and found a blueprint of Malthus's key. Keynes had ideas of his own, but he detected a kindred spirit in Malthus and proclaimed that Malthus's key was better than Ricardo's key, except that he had not completed it, so it was not able to open the safe. Ricardo, according to Keynes, was so carried away by his own key that he failed to take note of Malthus's key, even though the pair were the closest of friends and conversed and corresponded on ideas about keys for many years. Because Ricardo had his head in the clouds and because he was so well respected, nobody else took note of Malthus's key, either. Keynes claimed to have finished the blueprint, and with it he cracked open the safe and made the biggest splash since Adam Smith. There then ensued a heated debate over which came first: the (Keynes) chicken or the (Malthus) egg.

The point of the first part of this book is to demonstrate three things: (1) that there is another aspect to Malthus's blueprint that Keynes had not uncovered,[2] (2) that Ricardo was well aware of it (even though he disagreed with it), and (3) that it was a sound idea. It has been lying dormant for two centuries. I agree with Keynes that Malthus's blueprint is incomplete and that he wrote some contradictory things. Therefore, I cannot claim to have unearthed "the" true key, any more than Keynes could have; but the "signal" I describe is clearly extractible from the

DOI: 10.1057/9781137562210.0003

noise, even if it is not the exclusive pattern extractible from Malthus's writings. I select and I fill in gaps in Malthus's arguments (and I endeavor to point out to the reader each time I do so), but I do not believe that I fundamentally distort Malthus's ideas. That is what I meant when I wrote above that the idea sort of is, and sort of isn't novel.

The second part of this book updates Malthus's idea—which I call Accumulation—and applies it to explain the contemporary malaise of secular stagnation and boom-bust cycles in the United States. That is what this book is about.

2 Dramatis personae

Part I of this book is a recounting, analysis, and evaluation of the debate over the causes of economic growth, stagnation, and cycles between Thomas Robert Malthus and David Ricardo that took place through books, pamphlets, and copious correspondences in the 1810s to 1830s.[3] They were both Englishmen and during much of that time England was in a depression that followed on the end of the Napoleonic wars. Therefore, the question of what caused depression, what could cure it, and how permanent it might be, preoccupied both of them. Malthus is the better known of the two to the general public. His *Essay on the Principle of Population*—which has nothing whatever to do with the subject matter of this book—is one of the most recognized books in the English language. Among economists, however, Ricardo is a revered—if distant—figure, whereas Malthus's writings on economics are not part of the canon (even after Keynes attempted to resurrect his reputation). The intensity of both their friendship and their disagreements over economics is remarkable.

Jean Baptiste Say (1767–1832), a French contemporary and correspondent of Malthus and Ricardo, plays an important supporting role. One way of looking at the main theme of this book is through the lens of Say's claim that supply is a more fundamental economic activity than is demand. Say reasons that, because a buyer must offer something of value in exchange for the goods he purchases, a buyer is required to produce something of value—or to own a natural resource—with which to carry out the exchange. While it is money that is usually offered in exchange, the buyer must have previously offered something of value in order to obtain the money he uses to purchase goods. Most economists from Say's time to the present take Say's line of reasoning to imply that the

DOI: 10.1057/9781137562210.0003

sole motivation for engaging in the activity of producing goods for sale is to enable those so engaged to obtain the wherewithal to buy goods of their liking. That is what Say and Ricardo take it to mean. It accords with Adam Smiths's observation that "Consumption is the sole end and purpose of all production."[4] If Adam Smith is correct, then the only practical bound to output is the technological limits of production. That is why supply is a more fundamental economic activity than is demand.

Malthus disagrees; he thinks there are people—important people in his time—who produce for the purpose of accumulating productive power, money, and financial claims, without intending ever to convert their wealth into demand for final goods. The existence of such people, who sell, but never buy—whom I call accumulators in Chapter 3—creates a deficiency in demand, which prevents the economy from operating at full employment. If Malthus is correct, then aggregate demand plays a role in determining output and employment, even when wages and prices adjusted instantaneously to imbalances between supply and demand. The debate between Malthus and Ricardo concerns the question of whether Accumulation ever really takes place; Malthus says it does, and Ricardo says it does not. However, if Accumulation does take place, both agree that it will prevent the economy from attaining full employment.[5]

Adam Smith, "the" master safecracker, has a presence throughout this book for several reasons; because he wrote the first comprehensive description of the market economy as self-regulating system achieving spontaneous order through the feedback mechanism of the "invisible hand"; because he believed that production potential and not aggregate demand determined output, and because he railed—to good effect—against the evils of mercantilism. These are important topics of this book. The debate between Malthus and Ricardo takes place in the shadow cast by Adam Smith's ideas.

3 The core idea of this book

This book endeavors to explain the cause of secular stagnation, which I define to be a condition of low growth and underemployment of resources. It is shown that if an economically significant group saves a large portion of income it plans never to spend, the economy cannot operate at full employment on a sustainable basis. The conceptual tool

DOI: 10.1057/9781137562210.0003

that is used to establish and explain this result is the budget constraint faced by any person or institution (whom I call "agents"). In a simplified and highly aggregated form, the budget constraint faced by each agent is

$$\text{Prices} \times \text{goods} + \text{Wage} \times \text{labor services} + \text{Wealth} \equiv 0 \qquad (1.1)$$

If the agent is a net purchaser of an item, his amount will be positive, and if he is a net seller, his amount will be negative. It will be seen that (1.1) is an identity and that all transactions undertaken by any agent is represented in the budget constraint (as a subcomponent of a variable in (1.1)). The following thought experiment is undertaken. Prices are established and the agent formulates a plan to allocate his resources assuming that he will be able to carry out his planned transactions at the established prices. By aggregating the plans of all agents, it can be determined for each item whether, at the established prices, there is an excess amount of the item planned to be demanded or planned to be supplied. An equilibrium, or resting point of the economy, occurs when it attains a set of prices at which planned demand equals planned supply for each item.

There is an axiom in economic theory, called the non-satiation principle, which ensures that agents do not wish to acquire wealth; that they ultimately desire to spend all of their resources on goods.[6] An agent may save and acquire wealth at a point in time, but it is assumed that his plan is to spend the wealth on goods at some future dates.[7] If all agents behave in accordance with the non-satiation principle, the aggregate excess demand for wealth must always be zero, which implies that the aggregate excess demand for goods and labor must also always be zero. This does not ensure that there will be set of prices at which equilibrium is achieved, but it does rules out the possibility of an incurable excess supply of goods and labor.

An agent who plans to save and never to spend will accumulate wealth; his amount of wealth will be positive.[8] In order to pay for his acquisition of wealth, he must be a net seller of labor services and final goods. In Chapter 3 I define such an agent an "accumulator." An accumulator does not obey the non-satiation principle. If there are some accumulators in the economy, and if such agents plan to accumulate wealth no matter what the prices are, the economy will have an aggregate excess amount of planned sales of goods and labor. In this case, there will be an incurable excess supply of goods and labor, and the economy will operate below full employment of resources and it

DOI: 10.1057/9781137562210.0003

will not have an equilibrium. Such an economy will experience secular stagnation.

Malthus believed that the owners of merchant and manufacturing enterprises in his day—whom he called capitalists—were accumulators. His position is explored in Part I of this book. In Part II I argue, in the case of the United States, that offshore mercantilists—principally China—and top income earners have behaved as accumulators over the past two decades.

This framework can aid in the understanding of the tendency for economies experiencing Accumulation to suffer from cycles of investment boom and bust. Accumulators have an excess demand for wealth. If all budget constraints are adhered to, it will cause secular stagnation. But the real world is suffused in uncertainty that requires making guesses about how valuable capital assets will become in the future. Moreover, the excess saving of the accumulators drives down yields, which creates a temptation for all savers to look favorably on investments that promise a higher return. On the other side are entrepreneurs, punters, and gullible people who face the temptation to issue shares or borrow what is offered. Occasionally, there may appear a capital asset—such as houses—whose future value is overestimated by many people on both sides. As if by magic, an endowment of additional wealth appears, which expands budget constraints and allows people to spend more on goods and capital assets. When this occurred in the late 1990s and 2000s in the United States, labor was kept fully employed producing capital assets—such as laying fiber optic lines in the late 1990s and building houses in the mid-2000s—and by providing final goods to homeowners who had taken out loans collateralized by their homes. But when the future values failed to materialize, wealth melted away, which caused budget constraints to shrink, and secular stagnation to resume.

If the boom is financed by shares, that is all that will happen; and that is all that did happen after the dotcom boom of the late 1990s, which was financed by equity. The economy went into a mild recession followed by a "jobless" recovery. If the boom is financed by debt, however, the decline in the value of the collateral offered on loans will cause borrowers to become insolvent and banks—because they are highly leveraged—to also become insolvent and discontinue extending credit. The US housing boom of the 2000s was financed by massive debt and the recession that followed was the deepest and longest lasting since the Great Depression of the 1930s.[9]

DOI: 10.1057/9781137562210.0003

4 Relation to *The Financial Crisis Reconsidered*

Concurrent with the publication of this book, I have published a book on a related topic called *The Financial Crisis Reconsidered*.[10] It is a detailed study of the US housing boom of the 2000s and the financial crisis that followed it. Chapters 9 and 10 of that book articulate the idea of Accumulation and apply the concept to explain the causes of the volatility and secular stagnation the United States has experienced from the late 1990s to the present. Those chapters are the templates to Chapters 3 and 4, which form Part II of this book. There is no discussion of the history of idea of Accumulation in the *Financial Crisis* book, which is the subject of Part I of this book.

5 A note on methodology

The concept of Accumulation does not specify any particular outcome or time-path for economic variables. It establishes a boundary that delimits a space within which economic outcomes can occur when it is present. This may be unsatisfying to economists, who are trained to apply universal axioms of human behavior to particular environments in order to deduce explanations or predictions of more precise economic outcomes. But when events take place outside of equilibrium, and when there is no equilibrium toward which the economy gravitates, the standard approach may not be very useful in explaining events. Another way of looking at the matter is that Accumulation is a concept that does not require a great deal of institutional detail to apply. When, for example, China pursues a mercantilist policy to generate a current account surplus with the United States, the policy will have a depressing effect on the US economy regardless of the institutional structure and the expectations of US citizens. But that does not shed light on the channels through which China's policy affects events in the United States. With detailed information on those variables, the standard economic approach can be used to understand aspects of the course of events inside the United States. Any satisfactory understanding, however, will probably require the methods of the historian as much as that of the economist.

DOI: 10.1057/9781137562210.0003

Notes

1 Piero Sraffa, was an economist colleague of Keynes at Cambridge and who published the collected works of Ricardo, which include the letters between Ricardo and Malthus that are quoted at length in this book.
2 Lest the reader be misled that I have gone drunk with hubris, I note that the idea I extract is an order of magnitude less complex, less profound, and less generally applicable than what Keynes proposed.
3 There were countless hours of conversation as well, but none of that is available to us now.
4 Adam Smith, *The Wealth of Nations*, Modern Library Edition. New York: Random House Inc., 1994, p. 715.
5 This claim, which I substantiate in Chapter 1 with extensive quotations from Malthus and Ricardo, runs counter to almost all that has been written about the debate. It is likely to be the most controversial aspect of this book.
6 The non-satiation principle is introduced in Chapter 1.
7 This is an expression of the permanent income hypothesis, which is explained in Chapter 4.
8 Wealth is defined as money, financial claims—such as bank deposits, loans, equities, bonds and capital assets. See Table 2.1 in Chapter 2. Note also that the amount of wealth cannot be negative for any agent. Since agents are assumed to begin with no wealth they can only be net purchasers.
9 For a detailed analysis of the US housing boom and financial crisis, see Aronoff, Daniel (2016) *The Financial Crisis Reconsidered: The Mercantilist Origin of Secular Stagnation and Boom–Bust Cycles*. New York: Palgrave-Macmillan.
10 Ibid.

DOI: 10.1057/9781137562210.0003

Part I
The Malthus–Ricardo Debate

DOI: 10.1057/9781137562210.0004

1
The Malthus–Ricardo Debate on General Glut and Secular Stagnation

Abstract: *Adam Smith contends that a market economy gravitates to full employment and that its growth is limited only by the rate of capital accumulation and the cost of foodstuffs. JB Say asserts that demand is determined by supply; that people produce goods to obtain the means to make offerings to purchase the goods they desire. Thomas Malthus contends that capitalists do not produce goods in order to consume; they produce to accumulate wealth, which creates a deficiency in demand. Too high a rate of saving will render demand insufficient to support full employment. David Ricardo defends Adam Smith's position in his debate with Malthus. He and Malthus agree that the attainment of full employment hinges on whether people produce more than they plan to spend.*

Keywords: Adam Smith; aggregate demand; General Glut; Law of Markets; Malthus; Ricardo

Aronoff, Daniel. *A Theory of Accumulation and Secular Stagnation: A Malthusian Approach to Understanding a Contemporary Malaise*. New York: Palgrave Macmillan, 2016. DOI: 10.1057/9781137562210.0005.

> We have seen the powers of production, to whatever extent they may exist, are not alone sufficient to secure the creation of a proportionate degree of wealth. Something else seems to be necessary in order to call these powers fully into action. This is an effectual and unchecked demand for all that is produced...[1]
>
> It is unquestionably true that wealth produces wants; but it is a still more important truth that wants produce wealth.
>
> —Thomas R. Malthus[2]

> Virtue itself turns to vice being misapplied/And vice, sometimes by action dignified.
>
> —William Shakespeare[3]

1 Malthus's addition to Adam Smith's causes of the wealth of nations

In *The Wealth of Nations* (1776) Adam Smith enquires into the sources of economic prosperity and growth. He identifies two factors that fundamentally determine the prosperity and rate of growth of an economy. One factor is the degree to which the rule of law prevails—both the legal framework and obedience to it—which secures property rights and the sanctity of contracts necessary to promote the division of labor and the incentive to make capital investments. Smith describes a market economy as a self-regulating system governed by underlying forces generating supply and demand for each good. Participants in the market—whom I call "agents"—are led as if by "an invisible hand" to establish prices and a pattern of production that balance supply and demand for each good, and to effectuate a division of labor that expands output beyond what it would be if agents did not trade. Implicit in Smith's conceptualization is that a market economy tends to operate at full employment, since he assumes that human wants are insatiable which implies there is a profit to be earned by delivering (or transforming) an idle resource to someone who values it.[4] An economy in which planned (or *notional*) supply and demand for each good is balanced and all resources are utilized is in a state of "full employment equilibrium."[5] The other factor Smith identifies as contributing to prosperity and growth is the accumulation of capital—which requires that agents save

DOI: 10.1057/9781137562210.0005

and invest a portion of their income. Capital augments the productivity of labor, which expands potential output.[6]

According to Smith the rate of saving—for a given level of enforcement of property rights—is determined by the habit of parsimony, which is similar to what contemporary economists call the rate of time preference.[7] Smith contends that all planned saving is invested in capital:

> Whatever a person saves from his revenue he adds to his capital, and either employs it himself in maintaining an additional number of productive hands, or enables some other person to do so, by lending it to him for an interest that is, for a share of the profits.[8]

It follows that the more parsimonious citizens are, the greater will be the volume of capital accumulation and the rate of growth.

> Capitals are increased by parsimony, and diminished by prodigality and misconduct...[9]
>
> Parsimony, by increasing the fund which is destined for the maintenance of productive hands, tends to increase the number of those hands whose labor add to the value of the subject upon which it is bestowed. It tends therefore to increase the exchangeable value of the annual produce of the land and labor of the country. It puts into motion an additional quantity of industry, which gives an additional value to the annual produce.[10]

Smith believes that the habit of parsimony is, for the most part, a matter of innate character; and that the enterprises controlled by men of parsimonious habits are more likely to thrive and grow.[11]

> The principle which prompts to save, is the desire of bettering our condition, a desire which...comes with us from the womb, and never leaves us till we go into the grave.[12]

The assumption that a market economy gravitates to full employment equilibrium implies that the level and the rate of growth of output is determined by the size of the labor force, the state of technology (which determines the output—of foodstuffs and manufactured goods—achievable from a given combination of labor and capital), and the rate of saving. Those are the forces that determine potential output, and the gravitational pull toward full employment ensures that the economy will tend to operate at its potential output. Therefore, though demand plays a role in determining prices and production for individual goods—and consequently the allocation of resources—demand does not affect the aggregate level of output in Smith's system. This insight

DOI: 10.1057/9781137562210.0005

is more clearly articulated in the generation following Smith, by J. B. Say and James Mill, in the proposition that supply creates demand, since goods are required to be offered in exchange for goods and each individual produces only because of, and to the extent of, his demand for other goods.[13]

The growth of output of a market economy, as described by Adam Smith, is depicted in Figure 1.1. The horizontal axis represents time and the vertical axis represents the value of aggregate output at some base price index. Line *I-high* depicts the growth of output when saving (and investment) is "high," and line *I-low* when saving is "low." I-high lies above I-low because, as Smith explains, an economy becomes wealthier over time, the higher its rate of capital accumulation.

In Book II of the second edition of his *Principles of Political Economy* (1836), Malthus begins his enquiry into the determinants of the wealth of nations by asking why countries that are similar in respect of the two fundamental causal factors identified by Adam Smith nevertheless appear to differ in their levels of per capita output and rates of growth.

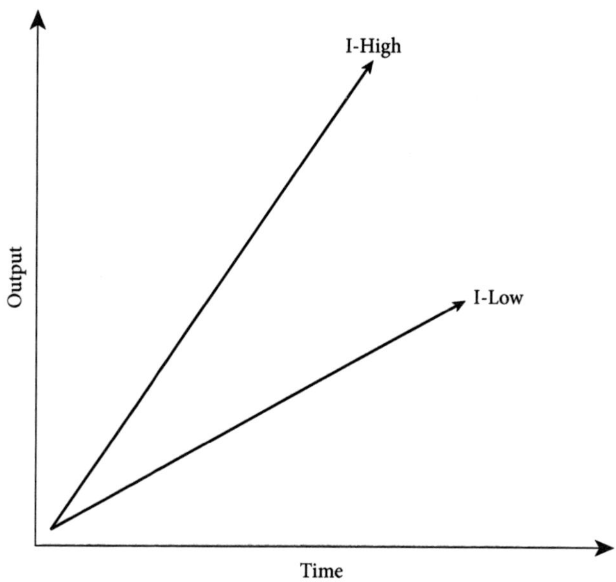

FIGURE 1.1 *The relation between investment and output over time in Adam Smith's model*

DOI: 10.1057/9781137562210.0005

> It is obviously true that there are many countries, not essentially different either in the degree of security which they afford to property, or in the moral and religious instruction received by the people, which yet, with nearly equal natural capabilities, make a very different progress in wealth... Whenever we take a view of the different states of Europe or the world... [we observe] countries with great powers of production comparatively poor, and countries with small powers of production comparatively rich.[14]

Malthus does not question Smith's view that capital investment is required to grow an economy. But he believes Smith fails to grasp that aggregate demand could exert an independent influence on employment, investment, and the growth of the economy over time.

> Adam Smith has stated, that capitals are increased by parsimony, that every frugal man is a public benefactor, and that the increase of wealth depends upon the balance of produce above consumption. That these propositions are true to a great extent is perfectly unquestionable... But it is quite obvious that they are not true to an indefinite extent, and that the principle of saving, pushed to excess, would destroy the motive to production. If every person were satisfied with the simplest food, the poorest clothing, and the meanest houses, it is certain no other sort of food clothing and lodging would be in existence.[15]

> If the actual riches of a country not subject to repeated violences and a frequent destruction of produce, be not after a certain period in some degree proportioned to its power of producing riches, **this deficiency must have arisen from the want of an adequate stimulus to continued production** [emphasis added].[16]

In treating aggregate demand as an independent causal factor, Malthus attempts to augment the Smithian paradigm by incorporating an explanatory variable he believes to have been overlooked. But the implication of positing aggregate demand as a causal factor in determining the state of the economy constitutes a radical departure from Smith's framework. It is difficult to convey just how upsetting Malthus's approach must have been on several different levels. The very concept of aggregate demand influencing employment contradicts the assumption that a market economy tends to operate a full employment.[17] It gives rise to the possibility that the invisible hand may leave resources or productive potential unused. It places the precepts of Christian morality in opposition to the necessities of material well-being. Many considered it blasphemy to assert that parsimony and thrift, by reducing aggregate demand, could force working men into unemployment, while prodigality and gluttony could restore their fortunes. This is the opposite of what Smith contended:

DOI: 10.1057/9781137562210.0005

> If the prodigality of some were not compensated by the frugality of others, the conduct of every prodigal, by feeding the idle with the bread of the industrious, tends not only to beggar himself, but to impoverish his country.[18]

Malthus's questioning of the benefits of parsimony and his belief in the importance of aggregate demand has antecedents. Bernard Mandeville, who was among the first social thinkers to realize the potential for divergence between individual motives and societal outcomes, wrote in the *Fable of the Bees* (1732) of how the reprobate traits of prodigality and avarice were sometimes beneficial to society, whereas frugality could bring on depression. Mandeville wrote of the unemployment and loss of wealth that could afflict a society where everyone behaved in accordance to Christian precepts. A diminution of prodigality would cause a collapse in demand, which would impoverish society.

> Frugality is like Honesty, a mean starving Virtue, that is only fit for small Societies of good peaceable Men, who are contented to be poor so they may be easy; but in a large stirring Nation you may have soon enough of it. 'Tis an idle dreaming Virtue that employs no Hands, and therefore very useless in a trading Country, where there are vast Numbers that one way or other must be all set to Work. Prodigality has a thousand Inventions to keep People from sitting still, that Frugality would never think of; and as this must consume a prodigious Wealth, so Avarice again knows innumerable Tricks to rake it together, which Frugality would scorn to make use of.[19]

Malthus was not alone in arguing that aggregate demand played a role in the economy. Among prominent contemporaries, Chalmers, Sismondi, and Lauderdale, espoused the view that a deficiency in aggregate demand could cause the economy to operate below its potential.[20] But Malthus singularly identified the sources of insufficient demand and articulated a logically coherent theory to explain its effect on the economy.

The attempt to incorporate aggregate demand into economic theory was violently resisted by Malthus's intellectual arch-rival David Ricardo, who was the most prominent and influential economist of the generation that followed Adam Smith. Ever since Malthus wrote of his ideas on demand, there has been a virtual consensus—even among his admirers—that he did not put forth a coherent theory. In contrast, Ricardo formulated in words a tight mathematical structure describing an economy in equilibrium. He cast the mould into which economic theory developed for the next hundred years, until the concept of aggregate demand re-emerged into the mainstream with the advent of the

DOI: 10.1057/9781137562210.0005

Keynesian revolution. It is argued in this and the next chapter that the consensus is right about Ricardo, but the assessment of Malthus is dead wrong.

2 Elements of Malthus's approach

In book II of his *Principles* (2nd Ed.), and in several of his letters to Ricardo, Malthus presents a clear, concise framework of the sources of, and consequences of, a shortfall in aggregate demand. In a nutshell, demand can fall short of the productive powers of an economy operating at full employment from any combination of the following reasons. A high rate of saving can cause an insufficient demand for final goods; consumers can become satiated with the manufactured goods on offer at less than full employment output if their variety is limited, and people rising out of poverty may not have cultivated the taste for luxuries and therefore may become satiated upon achieving a minimal standard of living, in which event they will limit their labor supply and choose to indulge in more leisure. Malthus argues that if any of these conditions apply, the economy will be forced to operate at below full resource utilization.

Malthus is one of the earliest economists to question what was the optimal amount to saving—that which could maximize consumption over time. It was a vexing problem given his (and Smith's) belief that saving behavior was influenced more by a fixed character trait, than by market forces. He raises a particular concern over whether the innate habit of parsimony described (and endorsed) by Smith might result in an excess of planned saving relative to profitable investment opportunities. If saving is not responsive to changes in interest rates and profits, there is no evident feedback loop to keep saving aligned with investment. According to Malthus, the excess of saving causes an insufficiency of demand for manufactured goods, which can periodically result in a glut of unsold final goods, in the event manufactures overestimate demand for future final goods.[21] The excess inventories cause the price of output to collapse, and both the decline in sales and price induces manufacturers to reduce output. The resultant increase in unemployment will cause "effectual" demand to contract further—because unemployed workers may have the "will," but lack the "power"—that is the wage income—to effectively demand

DOI: 10.1057/9781137562210.0005

goods—which can lead to another round of contraction of output and layoffs.

In accordance with common practice among writers on political economy at the time, Malthus conceptually divides society into three classes: capitalists, who own and operate merchant trading enterprises and manufacturing plants into which they make capital investments to increase capacity and to produce final goods output, and receive their income in the form of profits from the sale of final goods; landlords, who live on inherited estates that produce the foodstuffs necessary to support the population and earn their income in the form of rent; and workers, who labor in factories, in farming, and as service providers (mostly menial laborers to landlords, which is called "unproductive labor"[22]), and earn their income in the form of wages.[23] The important economic attribute of each group pertains to what they produce and how they divide their income between consumption and saving. Malthus posits that the members of each class divide their income between consumption and saving in accordance with different habits. Consumption, in turn, is divided between two types of goods: "necessaries," which include a culturally determined minimum amount of food and certain types of manufactured commodities; and luxuries, which are mostly comprised of manufactured commodities.[24] The way in which the economy distributes income among the three classes determines the aggregate volume of consumption. The patterns of income distribution between the classes, and consumption choices within them, affect the incentive to work and invest and the growth of output.

Workers have the highest propensity to consume when the wage is too low to cover necessaries, because, until their wage is sufficient to cover their necessities, they must spend all they earn in order for their families to survive. When the wage rises above the level at which it covers necessaries, Malthus believes that workers' propensity to consume (and to work) declines steeply, since they lack the cultivation of taste to desire luxuries.[25] Landlords consume a high proportion of their income on luxuries, because the technological possibilities to expand production of foodstuffs at a profit is limited by declining marginal productivity of land, and because they are educated to cultivate a taste for luxuries and they collect rent and have idle time.[26] Capitalists have a low propensity to consume because their chosen vocation self-selects for individuals who are willing to forego consumption in order to build an enterprise and amass wealth.

DOI: 10.1057/9781137562210.0005

Figure 1.2 depicts the consumption propensities (for families) of the three classes. The horizontal axis is income and the vertical axis is consumption. Yn is the level of income at which all necessaries can be purchased.[27]

According to Malthus, consumption growth requires a distribution of income between classes that supports a high-enough aggregate rate of consumption out of income to induce capitalists to maintain a high level of capital investment. This creates a tension. An elevated wage boosts aggregate consumption by shifting income share to high-spending workers (assuming that the wage is below the level required to pay for necessaries), but reduces the share of revenue that goes to profit. Above some wage level there is likely to be a trade-off between increased revenue and increased profit.[28] A reasonable rate of profit is necessary to induce capitalists to invest for two reasons: first, the fund for capital investment comes out of profits[29] and second, Malthus contends that capitalists will not invest their savings in capital if the rate of profit on new investment is too low. But the wage rate achieved in the market may not be compatible with a rate of profit on new investment sufficiently high to grow output

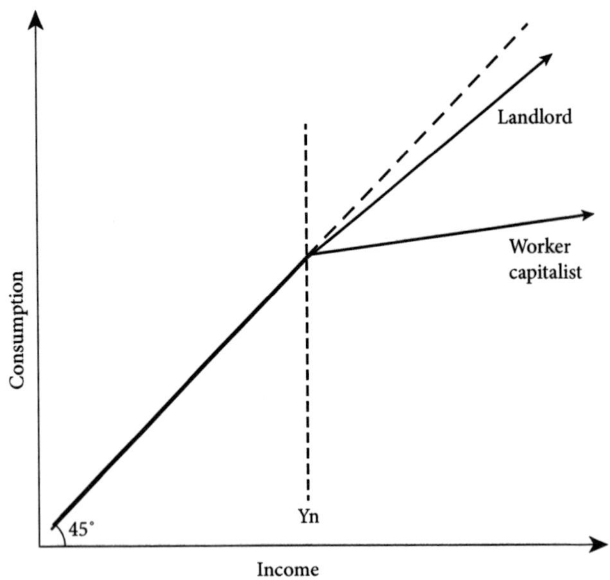

FIGURE 1.2 *The relation between income and consumption for different social classes in Malthus's model*

DOI: 10.1057/9781137562210.0005

capacity at a high rate over time.[30] In terms of Figure 1.1, the economy may be consigned to growth path I-*low*. Malthus notes the difficulty of balancing the need to generate demand with the need to encourage investment:

> To increase indeed, the proportion of the demand to the supply without a diminution of the produce is no easy task.[31]

This point can be explored further with the aid of Figure 1.3, which depicts the difference in aggregate income (which is the value of aggregate output) depending upon the share of income going to capitalists, assuming (1) a fixed volume of investment expenditure and (2) wages insufficient to cover all necessaries. In this figure, the vertical axis is aggregate expenditure—consumption and investment—and the horizontal axis is aggregate income. *Yf* represents aggregate income at full employment. Line *IE1* is the aggregate demand function when capitalists receive a "small" share of income. Line *IE2* is the aggregate demand function when capitalists receive a "large" share of income. *IE2* lies below *IE1* because, as can be seen in Figure 1.2, capitalists have a lower propensity to consume than any other group. The intersection

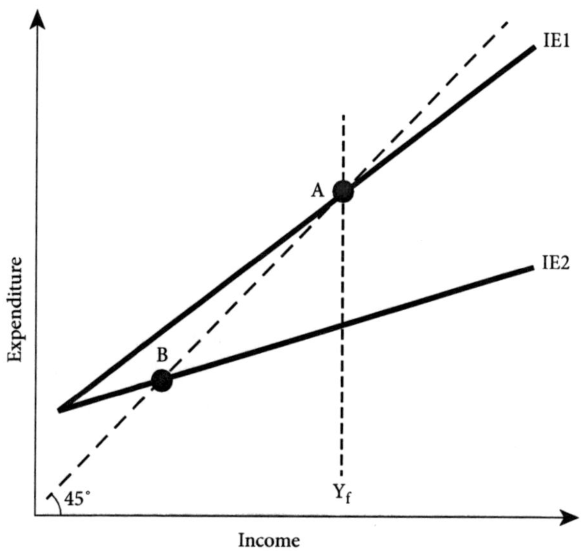

FIGURE 1.3 *The relation between income and expenditure assuming constant investment in Malthus's model*

DOI: 10.1057/9781137562210.0005

of the aggregate demand function and the 45° line represents the equilibrium point,[32] where aggregate income equals aggregate expenditure. Another way of understanding the 45° line is that along it saving equals investment. This can be readily apprehended by realizing that, in order for income to equal expenditure, the portion of income not spent on consumption must be spent on something else, and investment is the only alternative outlet. It represents the actual level of expenditure and income to which the economy tends.[33] It can be seen that output is higher at point A, the equilibrium when the capitalists' share of income is low, than it is at point B, the equilibrium when the capitalists' share of income is high.

It might appear from Figure 1.3 that the way to reach full employment if the economy is underutilizing its resources is to shift manufacturing income share to workers by increasing their wages. But that is only because the volume of investment is held constant. In reality, according to Malthus, investment will be influenced by profit. Beyond some wage level, the share of profit will decline to a level at which the increase in revenue is overtaken by the decline in profit share. Above that wage rate, investment will decline. It is therefore possible that the combined effects of capitalists' high-saving propensity and their need to earn a significant share of income required to motivate them to invest, will prevent the economy from operating at full employment.

This shows how strikingly Malthus's view of the consequences of saving behavior differs from Smith. The source of the difference needs to be understood. Both Smith and Malthus agree that investment increases growth and both agree that all actual (or effective) saving gets invested (the 45° line in Figure 1.3). Where they differ is that Malthus believes that too high a rate of planned saving is incompatible with full employment, because it will exceed investment—in fact, it will cause investment to fall. Too high a rate of planned saving will cause income (and employment) to contract to a lower level (point B in Figure 1.3) at which effective saving equals investment. Although they did not use the terms "notional" and "effective," in the substance of their arguments, it is evident that Malthus and Smith agree that, in actuality, all saving gets invested (an *effective* condition), but they differ as to whether planned saving always equals investment (a *notional* condition).[34] When planned saving exceeds the volume that can be profitably invested, it will cause output to contract by lowering demand for final goods; and the process will continue until desired saving declines to the level of investment.

DOI: 10.1057/9781137562210.0005

Malthus states the "paradox of thrift" a century before Keynes popularized the concept:

> [If] commodities are already so plentiful that an adequate portion of them is not profitably consumed, to save capital can only be still further to increase the plenty of commodities, and still further to lower already low profits, which can be comparatively of little use.
>
> National saving, therefore, considered as the means of increased production, is confined within much narrower limits than individual saving. While some individuals continue to spend, others individuals may continue to save to a very great extent; but the national saving, in reference to the whole mass of producers and consumers, must necessarily be limited by the amount which can be advantageously employed in supplying the demand for produce; and to create this demand, there must be an adequate and effective consumption either among the producers themselves, or other classes of consumers."[35]

The implication is that if saving is too high, employment and output will be forced to contract. For Malthus the problem is deeper that excess saving per se. The problem of under-consumption also arises from what Malthus calls an inadequate distribution of product; by which he means a lack of variety of manufactured goods of sufficient appeal to each of the social classes to prevent consumers from becoming satiated. This can arise from limitations in production technology and from limitations in consumers' tastes. Foreign trade can contribute to increasing consumption, according to Malthus, by introducing new goods that consumer's may desire. That desire may induce them to save less and to work more. Malthus expresses the importance of an adequate distribution of product to support consumption as follows;

> a continued increase in the value of the whole produce estimated in labor seems necessary to a continued and unchecked increase of wealth; because without such an increase of value it is obvious that no fresh labor can be set in motion. And in order to support this value it is necessary that an effective distribution of the produce should take place, and a due proportion be maintained between the objects to be consumed and the number, wants, and powers of the consumers, or, in other words, between the supply of commodities and the demand for them.[36]
>
> An increase in the quantity of produce depends chiefly upon the power of production, and an increase in the value of produce upon its distribution. Production and distribution are the two grand elements of wealth, which, combined in their due proportions, are capable of carrying the riches and population of the earth in no great length of time to the utmost limits of its possible resources; but which taken separately, or combined in undue proportions, produce only, after the lapse

> of many thousands of years, the scanty riches and scanty population, which are at present scattered over the face of the globe.[37]

To summarize, Adam Smith and his disciples believe that a well-functioning market economy tends toward full employment and that its growth is limited only by the size of labor force, the state of technology, and the rate of saving. Malthus, by contrast, contends that a market economy can be forced to operate at below full employment if either planned saving exceeds the quantity of profitable investment opportunities, or if the variety of final goods on offer fail to elicit consumer interest. When that occurs, the volume of investment will be reduced and the rate of output, employment, and growth will be below the trend that would obtain if the economy were to operate at full employment.

3 Malthus's model

Malthus does not map out any time-path of variables such as employment, output, investment, or growth as a stable function of other variables, such as saving propensities, capital stock, or technology. Nor does he identify any long-run resting point, or equilibrium of the economy as a function of specified variables. This places him at odds with the prevailing paradigm espoused by economists from Adam Smith to the present, whereby economic theory consists in the deduction of equilibrium outcomes (i.e. mutual adjustment of plans) derived from the application of certain axioms of human behavior operating in particular external environments. The type of theory economists strive for is modeled after the classical mechanics of 19th-century physics. Malthus's ideas do not readily fit into that mold. In the introduction to the second edition of his *Principles* Malthus explains his pluralistic methodology:

> In political economy the desire to simplify has occasioned an unwillingness to acknowledge the operation of more causes than one in the production of particular effects; and if one cause would account for a considerable portion of a particular class of phenomena, the whole has been ascribed to it without sufficient attention to the facts, which would not admit of being so solved.[38]

As a result of his openness to overdetermined causation and his disregard of an axiomatic approach to human motivation, Malthus's discussion of economic cycles and trend growth has been dismissed by economists as fragmentary journalistic descriptions of events

DOI: 10.1057/9781137562210.0005

lacking a sound theoretical foundation. In addition, as is discussed below, there was a consensus among mainstream economists (until the publication of Keynes's *General Theory*) that Malthus's concept of general glut contains a logical flaw because it is incompatible with the "law of markets."[39] Samuel Hollander, a leading scholar of classical economics, expressed this sentiment in a subtle and uncomplimentary way by commenting that "Malthus' general under-consumption or over-saving case is not easy to evaluate."[40] I think these dismissals overlook that in focusing on aggregate demand, Malthus was onto something of fundamental importance and truth, and that one aspect of his model is still overlooked by the majority of economists.[41] I contend that a careful reading of Malthus shows the dismissal of his ideas to be wrong. A coherent—if incomplete—theoretical model underlay Malthus's writings on employment, growth, and fluctuations. His approach can be usefully partitioned into two principle thematic components: economic cycles and trend growth.

Cycle: Malthus's description of a business cycle involves an oscillation between two opposing forces: a volume of final (manufactured) goods sales that is insufficient to absorb an increase in manufactured output, and the perennial drive of capitalists to expand manufactured output. He does not provide a clear account of what triggers an investment boom, but once it gets underway, workers are drawn from unproductive labor into manufacturing, where final goods output is expanded. Wages are not bid up (since Malthus claims to observe nominal wage stickiness). The fact that workers are merely shifted from one occupation to another with no increase in wages implies that there is no increase in demand for final goods. This results in an excess supply of manufactured goods. Malthus calls it a "general glut," which is a condition where large stocks of unsold inventories of all manufactured goods have accumulated. He describes what occurs this way:

> There would evidently be an unusual quantity of commodities of all kinds in the market, owing to those who had been before engaged in personal services having been converted, by the accumulation of capital, into productive laborers; while the number of laborers altogether being the same, and the power and will to purchase for consumption among landlords and capitalists being by supposition diminished,[42] commodities would necessarily fall in value compared with labor, so as very greatly to lower profits, and to check for a time further production.[43]

The dynamic of boom to bust is depicted in Figure 1.4, where the horizontal axis is the quantity of aggregate manufactured goods and the

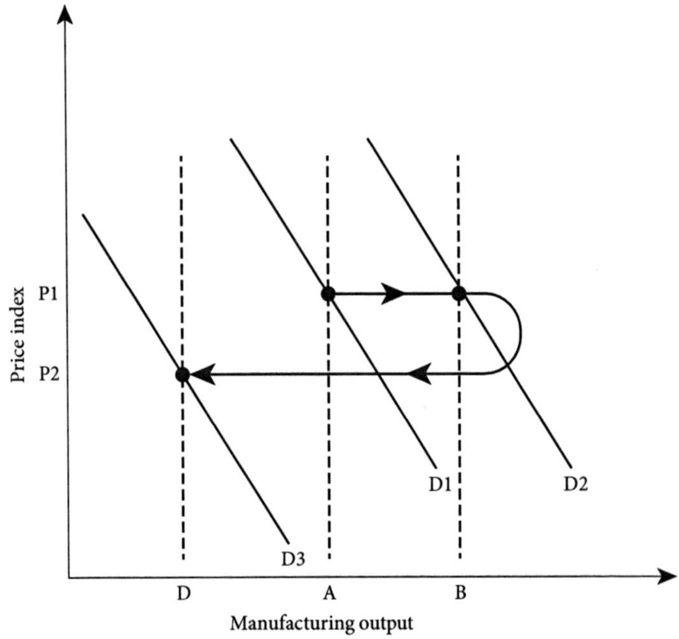

FIGURE 1.4 *The movement of output and prices in Malthus's short-term cycle*

vertical axis is an index of the aggregate price of manufactured goods. Manufacturing output is initially at volume A, on demand curve D1, and the price index is at P1. Then there is a perceived increase in demand and capitalists perceive the demand curve to shift from D1 to D2. This results in a perceived excess demand of (B–A) manufactured goods. Malthus does not say what triggers the perceived shift in demand, but he is clear that the relevant demand is a demand for future goods. And since it is uncommon for buyers to contract in advance for future delivery of goods, I think it is justifiable to assume that Malthus considered the outward shift in demand to be an expectation held by capitalists (hence it is perceived, rather than observed). Labor is then drawn into manufacturing and output expands to B, but the demand does not materialize. This results in an unsold glut of goods, measured by (B–A).

Next, goods prices fall below the cost of production—from P1 to P2—which renders capitalists unwilling or unable to continue to produce goods that either cannot be sold or cannot be produced at a profit. The contraction that follows is driven by two forces. One source of contraction is the reaction of capitalists to curtail final goods production and convert their income into unspent saving (in the form of money or loans). According to Malthus:

> It is equally vain, with a view to the permanent increase of wealth, to continue converting revenue into capital, when there is no adequate demand for the products of such capital, as to continue encouraging marriage and the birth of children without a demand for labor and an increase in the funds for its maintenance.[44]

The curtailment of investment reduces output below A (after inventories have been sold off). But there is another source of reduction in demand; it is that unemployed workers lack the income to demand goods, which implies that aggregate demand is below the level at which it was at the beginning of the cycle. The demand curve has shifted to D3, and demand will stay below volume A until unemployed manufacturing workers are able to find employment in the unproductive sector.

Malthus does not explain what occurs after the onset of recession, or how unemployed labor moves back into unproductive employment, setting up the next cycle. There is no formal role for expectations and, other than asserting that an increase in perceived demand initiates an overproduction of manufactured goods, there is no explicit sequence of events. These gaps in his explanation are one reason why many scholars are dismissive of Malthus's ideas. It should be kept in mind, however, that Malthus is describing events which take place outside of equilibrium, where plans are incompatible and expectations are disappointed. One way to model behavior in this situation is to assume that there is an equilibrium that acts as an attractor toward which the economy gravitates. It is how Ricardo and almost all economists after him have approached the matter. Yet, if Malthus's reasoning is correct, the structural deficiency in final goods demand makes full employment equilibrium impossible to attain and it may deprive the economy of any equilibrium at all. To this day, nobody has figured out a satisfactory way of describing the behavior of the economy in a situation like that.

Ricardo conjectures that the glut will be prevented by an increase in wages which he thinks would be required to attract labor into manufacturing (Ricardo's ideas are addressed below). If wages rise, Ricardo reasons that workers' high rate of consumption will maintain demand for the increased manufacturing output. Malthus argues two points in rebuttal. One is that capitalists will only employ labor to the extent they project making a profit, which implies a portion of expected earnings

DOI: 10.1057/9781137562210.0005

must be paid to capitalists, who are (he supposes) constitutionally disposed to spend very little of it on final goods. The other reason is that he believes the working class possesses a limited appetite for luxury goods (in the short term), so that if the wage rises above the level at which it covers payment of necessaries, workers will either save their earnings or withdraw from the labor market. That leaves landlords to fill the consumption void, which requires their share of income to increase. But there is no prima facie reason to suppose the market will generate that outcome.[45]

There is nothing unusual or remarkable in the idea that a business cycle is triggered by an overinvestment boom. In Chapter 4 the Wicksell/Hayek business cycle theory is discussed, which is a frequently cited approach to conceptualizing business cycles, in which the cycle starts with an investment boom. However, Malthus's account differs from many other accounts of the business cycle in one respect; in his account the boom is undermined by a deficiency in final goods demand, not by increased interest rates or inflation. In conventional accounts it is almost always the other way round; there is so much demand generated during the boom that interest rates and inflation spike upward—and that is what ultimately ends the boom. It is explained below how Malthus's account of the business cycle is cognate with the most plausible framework in which to understand the US housing boom of the 2000s and the recession that followed.

Trend: Malthus asserts that the proclivity of capitalists to accumulate—i.e. to permanently abstain from consuming most of their income above the level required to provide for necessaries—is a fixed behavioral trait.[46] It is not a flexible attitude that adjusts in response to market forces so as to increase consumption when that is necessary to ensure full employment and growth.

> [Capitalists] have certainly the power of consuming their profits, or the revenue which they make by the employment of their capitals ... But such consumption is not consistent with the actual habits of the generality of capitalists.[47]

Malthus argues that capitalists' high-savings rate, in combination with their sizeable share of income, creates a secular deficiency in demand for final goods. In terms of Figure 1.3, it pushes the economy to point B, below full employment (except during the boom phase of a cycle). By reducing final goods sales, the high-saving rate reduces the profit on capital investment, which causes output to contract both by reducing

DOI: 10.1057/9781137562210.0005

the incentive to invest and the funds available to invest. In terms of Figure 1.1, it pushes the economy onto the low growth path *I-min*. A high rate of saving is not the only cause of a deficiency in demand. As discussed above, a dearth of goods capable of eliciting desire from consumers—beyond some quantity—can be an independent source of deficient demand.

There is no easy solution to the problem of deficient demand. Malthus does not call for redistribution of capitalists' income because he recognizes that those people must be given the financial incentive to carry out investment and production.[48] As shall be demonstrated in Chapter 2, the assertion that capitalists intend not to spend on final goods a large portion of what they save—which I define as Accumulation—throws into disarray many cherished tenants of economic theory. It prevents the economy from maintaining full employment equilibrium by violating the non-satiation principle for goods, which is the proposition that every person always desires an additional increment of least some final good. A process that does not hone in on equilibrium is chaotic and unpredictable. For this reason economists have not been able to fit Accumulation into their models.

As with his description of the cycle, Malthus cites the deficiency in demand induced by the high-saving propensity of capitalists as one (but not the exclusive) driving force behind secular stagnation. And as with the cycle, it shall be explained in Chapter 3 how Malthus's account of secular stagnation is cognate with the most plausible framework in which to understand the low employment and low growth suffered by the US economy from the late 1990s to the present time.

4 Malthus's debate with Ricardo

Malthus debated his ideas on growth and stagnation (and much else) with David Ricardo. I partition Ricardo's (and, in some instances, J. B. Say's) responses to Malthus on these topics into cycle, trend, and the channel by which money affects output.

Cycle: Ricardo disagrees with Malthus's contention that the process of increasing output of manufactured goods will cause a deficiency in demand and ultimately a decline in employment. He believes that the economy will gravitate back to full employment whenever it is pushed away from it. The differences in their positions stem from a

DOI: 10.1057/9781137562210.0005

disagreement concerning two matters: the degree of wage flexibility in the economy and the spending habits of capitalists. Ricardo employs two arguments to counter Malthus's contention. First, starting from a position of full employment and no inventories, he reasons that capitalists will have to bid up the wage to entice workers to leave unproductive employment to work in factories. This will shift income away from capitalists—by reducing their profit share—in favor of labor. The higher propensity to consume of workers will provide demand for the increased output, which will ensure that capitalists continue to make profits, even as their profit share is eroded. So long as capitalists continue to make profits they will continue to produce. Second, starting from a position of a glut of unsold inventories, Ricardo argues that capitalists will scale back production and increase their final goods consumption, while the price of inventories and the wage rate will both decline to clear excess supplies (of goods and labor). These adjustments will cause output price and capitalist profit share both to rise, which will convince capitalists to re-hire labor in order to scale up production. Ricardo states his position as follows:

> I acknowledge there may not be adequate motives for production, and therefore things will not be produced, but I cannot allow, first that with these inadequate motives commodities will be produced, and secondly that, if their production is attended with loss to the producer, it is for any other reason than because too great a proportion is given to the laborers employed. Increase their number, and the evil is remedied. Let the employer consume more himself, and there will be no diminution of demand for labor, but the pay of the laborer, which was before extravagantly high, will be reduced.[49]

Malthus claims to observe that wages adjust sluggishly to changes in labor demand and on that basis he doubts that the wage will adjust to clear the labor market.[50] Ricardo assumes that wages must adjust rapidly, since, he reasons, it is in the interest of workers to make the adjustment. The disagreement over wage flexibility underlies their divergent conclusions about the degree to which wages will rise, and cause consumption to increase during periods of expansion; and fall, thereby increasing capitalists' profits, during periods of contraction.[51]

Malthus's belief that capitalists are pre-programmed for parsimony, implies they will not increase their consumption in response to a decline in profits. Ricardo, on the other hand, assumes that capitalists will curtail their saving and increase consumption when the return on investment

DOI: 10.1057/9781137562210.0005

declines, since that adjustment in behavior appears to be the optimizing thing to do. Ricardo states;

> [The] motive for accumulation will diminish with every diminution of profit, and will cease altogether when [capitalists] profits are so low as not to afford them an adequate compensation for their trouble, and the risk which they must necessarily encounter in employing their capital productively.[52]

On these differences of opinion rests their divergent conclusions about the ability of the economy to return to full employment equilibrium after a general glut has occurred. If, as Malthus contends, wages and spending habits remain inflexible, or adjust sluggishly in response to an excess supply of labor and inventories, there is no evident mechanism by which employment will increase. But if, as Ricardo contends, wages decline to clear the labor market, and capitalists adjust their habits to spend more of their income on final goods or menial labor (who, in turn, will spend their wages on goods), it is plausible that the economy will move toward full employment.[53]

Malthus and Ricardo both concern themselves with short-term dynamics; they understand each other's position and they each rely upon their perception of how markets actually behave. They disagree about two things: the degree of wage flexibility and the fixity of capitalists' low propensity to consume. These matters determine whether or not the economy hones in on full employment equilibrium. This point of view differs from the opinion of many scholars, who believe that Malthus is focused on short-term dynamics while Ricardo has his mind on long-run equilibrium, and that Malthus pays attention to facts, while Ricardo is buried in abstract theory.[54] That is not evident from Ricardo's comments above. The mis-perception may have its origin in a comment Ricardo himself wrote to Malthus:

> It appears to me that one great cause of our difference of opinion, on the subjects which we have so often discussed, is that you have always in your mind the immediate and temporary effects of particular changes—whereas I put these immediate and temporary effects quite aside and fix my whole attention on the permanent state of things which will result from them.[55]

In any event, Ricardo's statement is belied by his engagement with immediate "temporary" issues in his exchange with Malthus and his championing of short term considerations over long term consequences in debates over corn law and poor law reform.[56]

DOI: 10.1057/9781137562210.0005

Trend: A fundamental proposition put forth by Adam Smith is that all income is spent. It is either used to purchase capital or final goods by the recipient, or paid to laborers (which is income to them), or is lent out to others, who use it to either purchase goods or to pay laborers.

J. B. Say builds on Smith's insight to formulate the proposition that any market transaction requires that a party demanding some good must provide a good of equal value in exchange. In his *Traité d'économie politique* (1814) he observes that "la production qui ouvre des débouchés aux produits."[57] This insight was repeated in his *Letters to Malthus* (1921) in which he states:

> ...we purchase commodities with productive services, and...the more productive services we carry to market, the more we can buy in return.[58]
>
> All the producers possess collectively the means of acquiring the whole of the productions.[59]

The proposition that goods are produced for the sole purpose of creating the means to pay for other goods, that is to provide an effective demand for goods, lies at the foundation of what has come to be known—in varied and contentious permutations—as "Say's Law."[60] In his *Principles of Political Economy and Taxation* (Chapter XXI) Ricardo amplifies the argument that demand is limited only by the capacity to produce:

> M. Say has, however, most satisfactorily shewn, that there is no amount of capital which may not be employed in a country, because demand is only limited by production. No man produces but with a view to consume or sell, and he never sells, but with an intention to purchase some other commodity, which may be immediately useful to him, or which may contribute to future production. By producing, then, he necessarily becomes either the consumer of his own good, or the purchaser and consumer of the goods of some other person.[61]

Neither Say nor Ricardo deny there can be gluts of particular commodities, but they understand the condition as a temporary disequilibrium phenomena.[62] Say denies outright that there can be a general glut (i.e. an excess supply of all goods). He reasons that an excess supply of one good must be matched by an equal excess demand for other goods. "...if certain goods remain unsold it is because other goods are not produced."[63] As is explained in Chapter 2, this proposition—which is called Say's Principle—follows from the assumption that, at given market prices, the value of goods (including money and financial claims) a person plans to purchase, equals the revenue the person anticipates receiving from goods (including money and financial claims) he exchanges or sells (which can

DOI: 10.1057/9781137562210.0005

include his labor). Say's proposed solution is to increase production of the goods experiencing an excess demand, which will provide to sellers of those goods the money to that will enable them to purchase the goods experiencing excess supply: "To buy the super-abundant produce it would be requisite to create other produce."[64] Say does not believe a market operating without government interference will produce a persistent glut (though he allows for a temporary partial glut that will quickly be remedied). He lays blame for the persistent underproduction of goods in excess demand on distortionary taxation that discourages the production of those goods, and he prescribes the elimination of the offending taxes, in order to incentivize capitalists to produce the goods required to restore equilibrium.[65]

Ricardo admits of the possibility of a general glut. He argues, however, that any overproduction is a result of errors in judgment by capitalists.[66] "Men err in their productions...there is no deficiency in demand."[67] He believes that the market will operate in such a way that the goods in excess supply will be sold off (at below the cost of production, if necessary) and that capitalists will re-allocate production to become aligned with demand.[68] The reason he offers for denying the possibility of a persistent general glut—or secular stagnation—gets to the heart of his disagreement with Malthus:

> Adam Smith has justly observed "that the desire of food is limited in every man by the narrow capacity of the human stomach, but the desire of the conveniences and ornaments of building, dress, equipage, and household furniture, seems to have no limit or certain boundary"...and while there is no limit to the desire of "conveniences, ornaments of building, dress, equipage, and household furniture," there can be no limit to the capital that may be employed in procuring them, except that which bounds our power to maintain the workmen who are to produce them...[69]
>
> It follows from these admissions that there is no limit to demand—no limit to the employment of capital while it yields any profit, and that however abundant capital may become, there is no other adequate reason for a fall of profit but a rise of wages, and further it may be added, that the only adequate and permanent cause for the rise of wages is the increasing difficulty of providing food and necessaries for the increasing number of workmen.[70]

As discussed above, economists of Malthus and Ricardo's time divided goods into two categories: necessaries and luxuries. Necessaries were thought to be culturally determined, so they extend beyond the "stomach" in rich countries, but they are finite. The crucial assumption is that

DOI: 10.1057/9781137562210.0005

the human appetite for luxuries is insatiable, which economists call the "non-satiation principle." As long as there are unmet wants there will be a market in which to sell final goods; and since the supplier of goods has wants, too, he demands goods in exchange. Supply *creates* demand. That is the law of markets. And the only limiting factor is technological; in Ricardo's time it was perceived to be the declining marginal productivity of agriculture. The economy tends to full employment because idle resources—including labor—can be utilized to create goods that can be exchanged for other goods that will satisfy (but not satiate) the wants of people. In his discussion of general glut, Ricardo recognizes that, were the non-satiation principle not to obtain, there could be a permanent general glut:

> If every man were to forego the use of luxuries and be intent only on accumulation, a quantity of necessaries might be produced for which there could not be any immediate consumption. Of commodities so limited in number, there might undoubtedly be an universal glut; and consequently there might neither be demand for an additional quantity of such commodities, nor profits on the employment of more capital. **If men ceased to consume, they would cease to produce** [emphasis added].[71]

This, as shown above, is precisely the reason Malthus gave for his prognosis of secular stagnation—that capitalists are "intent only on accumulation." Ricardo concedes that a general glut may occur, but he discounts the possibility of a permanent general glut by affirming the non-satiation principle:

> This admission does not impugn the general principle. In such a country as England, for example, it is difficult to suppose that there can be any disposition to devote the whole capital and labor of the country to the production of necessaries only.[72]

Malthus recognizes that Ricardo has put his finger on the fundamental issue the divides them and he responds vigorously:

> Mr. Ricardo then adds, "This admission does not impugn the general principle." In the last remark I can by no means agree with him. It appears to me most completely to impugn the general principle.[73]

Malthus lodges three reasons why men may "cease to consume" for a protracted period of time. First, he points out that one possible reaction to higher wages—an increase in population (which might cause wages to fall and profits to rise as the demand for necessaries increases)—will

DOI: 10.1057/9781137562210.0005

only add to the labor force decades into the future. Second, workers may prefer indolence (or what we now call leisure) over luxuries, which will reduce labor supply while causing the deficiency in demand for luxuries to persist. Third, capitalists will go on saving even in the presence of glut:

> It has also been said, that there is never an indisposition to consume, that the indisposition is to produce. Yet, what is the disposition of those master manufacturers, and merchants who produce very largely and consume sparingly?[74]

But capitalist saving will not translate into demand because the low profits will cause them to contract employment.

> An accumulation, to a certain extent, of common food and clothing might take place on both sides; but the amount must necessarily be extremely confined. It would be no sort of use to the farmer to go on cultivating his land with a view merely to give food and clothing to his laborers... It would still be more useless to the manufacturers to go on producing clothing beyond what was wanted by the agriculturalists and themselves....there would evidently therefore be a general want of demand, both for produce and population.[75]

Finally, Malthus squarely identifies the "non-satiation" principle as the fundamental issue upon which their views diverged:

> But to come to a still more specific and fundamental cause of our difference, I think it is this. You seem to think that the wants and tastes of mankind are always ready for the supply; while I am most decidedly of opinion that few things are more difficult than to inspire new tastes and wants... I am quite of the opinion that **practically** the actual check to produce and population arises more from want of stimulus than want of power to produce.[76]

Once again, it is evident that Malthus and Ricardo understand the issue that divides them; it is the applicability of non-satiation. It is explained in Chapter 2 that the non-satiation principle ensures that all income received is eventually spent on final goods. Malthus's contention that capitalists spend less than they earn, and that workers and other may have a limited demand for final goods, constitutes a violation of the non-satiation principle. It is the fundamental source of deficient demand identified by Malthus.

Money: Malthus and Ricardo understand that the demand for, and supply of money could exert an influence on economic activity. Ricardo believes that money affects the economy only in the short term, as prices transition from one equilibrium level to the next. He

DOI: 10.1057/9781137562210.0005

does not consider a change in the demand for money, since he believes that money is held only for the purpose of having enough on hand to complete planned transactions. He does, however, allow that a change in the supply of money will have an immediate effect on the demand for goods. For example, a decrease in the supply of money will initially cause a contraction in purchases of goods. But the effect will be short lived, and the economy will return to full employment equilibrium when prices have declined in proportion to the decrease in the money supply. Ricardo writes:

> ...a reduction in the amount of the circulating medium should speedily operate on prices, but the resistance which is offered—the unwillingness that every man feels to sell his goods at a reduced price, induces him to...postpone the necessity of selling. The effect [of price reductions] is however certain at last, but duration of the resistance...cannot be the subject of anything like accurate calculation.[77]

Ricardo is a precursor of monetarism. The quoted passage resonates with Milton Friedman's description of money acting on the economy with long and variable lags, while neutral in the long run.

Malthus, at least in a few passages, identifies the interest rate as the crucial conduit of influence linking money to the economy, as the price that mediates saving and investment. His description of the effect of an excess of saving over investment when interest rates reach their lower bound, which was taking place in England at the time of his writing, is a precursor to the concept of the Keynesian liquidity trap:[78]

> The fall in the interest on money and the difficulty of finding employment for capital are universally acknowledged, and this fact, none of your friends have ever accounted for in any tolerably satisfactory manner.[79]

The following passage from Say's letter to Malthus, echoes Malthus's view and contrasts it with Ricardo's position.

> Mr. Ricardo insists that...there is always as much industry as capital employed; and that all capital saved is always employed, because interest is not suffered to be lost. On the contrary, many savings are not invested, when it is difficult to find employment for them, and many which are employed are dissipated in ill-calculated undertakings.[80]

The difference between Malthus and Ricardo's view of money can be stated as follows. If all desired saving is always invested; in the long run the interest rate will equal the rate of time preference, adjusted for risk no matter what are the monetary conditions. That is Ricardo's view. If, on the other hand, it is allowed that desired saving can exceed investment, the interest rate set by the supply and demand for money can affect the volume of investment (even, it should be noted, if the rate of saving does not change). And if, at the lower bound of interest rates, desired saving still exceeds investment, the economy will contract. That is Malthus's view.

5 The salient differences between Malthus and Ricardo

Malthus and Ricardo both agree that a general gut and mass unemployment can occur in the short run. Ricardo contends that glut and unemployment are disequilibrium phenomena that are caused by human error. He believes there is always, in principle, a full employment equilibrium; that the economy hones in on equilibrium and that wages, prices, saving habits, and production schedules rapidly adjust so as to effectuate the movement to equilibrium. The motive for adjustment, he posits, is that people are ever ready to change course and ignore traditions order to optimize their prospects. This reflects the temperament and outlook of a stock broker in the City of London.

Malthus believes people display behavioral patterns that are relatively fixed (or at least they change slowly over time). This includes the spending habits of the different classes of society. The "general object" of a capitalist is to "save a fortune" and workers lack the cultivation to desire luxuries. These parsimonious habits cannot be changed overnight. Likewise, the human relationship element in wage setting sets precedents that are not easily changed. This reflects the temperament and outlook of a country clergyman.

The deepest division between Malthus and Ricardo—which they both recognize—concerns the question of whether or not the non-satiation principle always obtains. On this matter rests the possibility that aggregate demand can determine the level of output, even where agents optimize and wages and prices are flexible. Where Ricardo states: "No man produces but with a view to consume or sell and he never sells, but with an intention to purchase some other commodity," Malthus responds (in effect) that capitalists produce and sell without any intention to purchase another commodity.

DOI: 10.1057/9781137562210.0005

Notes

1 Malthus, Thomas R. (1836) *Principles of Political Economy, second edition*, reprinted by August M. Kelley, New York (1964), p. 361.

2 Ibid., p. 403.

3 *Romeo and Juliet* Act 2, Scene 3.

4 Note that the "idle resource" can be unemployed labor.

5 Neither Smith, Malthus, nor Ricardo—whose ideas are discussed in this chapter—used this phrase, but their writings display an implicit recognition of the concept of full employment equilibrium. It is the state toward which Smith and Ricardo believe a market economy hones in on; and it defines the state Malthus feels the economy may fall short of. Since the phrase is familiar to the contemporary reader, I shall freely use it in discussing the ideas of these economists.

6 The state of technology is an implicit factor involved in prosperity and growth. It imposes limits on the variety, quality, and achievable level of output.

7 The term "time preference" refers to the rate of discount of future consumption versus current consumption. Economists assume this rate to be positive. A low rate of time preference is associated with patience and a willingness to defer consumption into the future, even if the yield earned on investment is low. The concept of time preference was not available to Adam Smith, but his description of parsimony is congruent to the concept. A parsimonious person, who is willing to forego consumption in order to save and invest, has a low rate of time preference.

8 Smith, Adam (1776) *The Wealth of Nations*, republished by Random House Inc., Modern Library edition, 1994, p. 368.

9 Ibid., p. 367.

10 Ibid., p. 368. I contend that this passage (and others) show that Smith has in mind the concept of planned saving—that is intended saving at full employment equilibrium—since nowhere does he consider the possibility that a high rate of saving could cause output, income (and, hence actual saving) to fall.

11 Smith does describe one circumstance in which parsimony is affected by market prices. A high rate of profit will satiate the desire to accumulate wealth and cause people to devote a greater portion of their income to consumption: "The high rate of profit seems every where to destroy that parsimony which in other circumstances is natural to the character of the merchant. When profits are high, that sober virtue seems to be superfluous, and expensive luxury to suit better the affluence of his situation." Moreover, the example set by "the owners of the great mercantile capitals" influences

DOI: 10.1057/9781137562210.0005

the habits of their workers; "If his employer is attentive and parsimonious, the workman is very likely to be so too; but if the master is dissolute and disorderly, the servant who shapes his work according to the pattern which his master prescribes to him, will shape his life too according to the example which he sets him." Smith, Adam (1776) *The Wealth of Nations*, republished by Random House Inc., Modern Library edition, 1994, p. 662.

12 Smith, *The Wealth of Nations*, p. 372.

13 In a monetary economy, goods are not traded for other goods, but rather for money. Yet, Smith and most other economists before Keynes believe that money is a veil, held merely for the purpose of facilitating multilateral exchanges of goods or to accommodate staggered timing of transactions, except in times of distress, when money is held as a precaution.

14 Malthus, *Principles of Political Economy*, , p. 310.

15 Ibid., pp. 6–7.

16 Ibid.

17 Full employment generates the upper bound of output. Aggregate demand cannot cause the economy to defy the laws of physics and exceed its upper bound. Therefore, the only circumstances in which aggregate demand can influence the level of output is when the economy is operating below full employment.

18 Smith, *The Wealth of Nations*, , p. 369.

19 Mandeville, Bernard (1732) *The Fable of The Bees or Private Vices, Publick Benefits*, reprinted by the Liberty Fund, Indianapolis, 1988, p. 106.

20 See Sowell, Thomas (1974) *Classical Economics Reconsidered*. Princeton, NJ: Princeton University Press, pp. 50–51.

21 A "final good" is a manufactured good intended for consumption. It is contrasted with a "capital good," which is a good that is used in the process of manufacturing a final good. See the discussion and application of these concepts in Chapter 2.

22 Following Adam Smith, Malthus's use of the term "unproductive labor" is not pejorative. It does not imply that such workers do nothing useful. It is merely a term to distinguish the type of work they do from the production of reproducible manufactured goods.

23 Malthus and Ricardo assume there is a single wage for workers toward which all wages gravitate. I use the term "wage" to refer to that single wage. However, I sometimes use the term "wages" when discussing the dynamics of adjusting wage rates, since the rate of change is subject to individual or independent group wage bargains.

24 I define "goods" to comprise all objects of consumption and investment. It excludes financial claims and money. Luxuries also include some imported goods, but I ignore foreign trade in this exposition.

DOI: 10.1057/9781137562210.0005

25 According to Malthus, this applies only in the short term. In the long term, if wages remain above subsistence, workers will become acquainted with luxuries and acquire a taste for them.

26 Malthus writes that the very richest landlords do save quite a lot, and invest in capitalist enterprises. But since the limited liability corporation had not been invented at the time of his writing, there was practically a much more limited range of investments that a person could consider than would become the case after the passage by the UK Parliament of the Limited Liability Act of 1855. Therefore, I ignore the possibility that landlords could invest a portion of their profits in manufacturing without (I think) compromising the analysis.

27 To simplify the exposition, Figure 2.2 applies to one period (say, a year) and ignores that prior saving can be used to purchase necessities.

28 The trade-off can be modeled by a simple profit formula. Ignoring the rental cost of capital and depreciation, profit can be represented by the equation:

$$\Pi = S(w) - wL$$

where Π represents profit; S(w) is sales, which is an increasing function of the wage (w), and L is the employed labor force. Holding employment constant, the first-order condition is:

$$d\pi/dw = S'(w) - w.$$

The first term on the left is positive and the second term is negative. If it is further assumed that low profits will cause capitalists to pull back on current output (and employment), then consumption (and revenue) will actually decline above some wage level, and the second moment, S'(w) will be negative, which may cause the profit rate first to rise, and then fall, as the wage increases.

29 This can include prior accumulated profits held in the form of money, financial claims, final good inventories, and capital.

30 In fact, there may not be any wage compatible with a maximization of technologically feasible consumption over time.

31 Malthus, *Principles of Political Economy*, p. 371.

32 Note that equilibrium, in terms of equality of income and expenditure does not imply notional equilibrium, nor (obviously) does it imply full employment.

33 The economy is not stable at any point where aggregate income and expenditure diverge. For the economy as a whole (though not necessarily for each individual) what is earned is, by definition what is spent. And what is spent must, by definition, come from what is earned.

34 The terms “notional” and “actual” correspond to the terms “ex ante” and “ex post” as commonly used by economists.

35 Malthus, *Principles of Political Economy*, p. 401.

36 Ibid., p. 365.

DOI: 10.1057/9781137562210.0005

37 Ibid., p. 371.

38 Ibid., p. 5.

39 The law of markets refers to the idea that planned supply and demand for final goods are always in balance. The concept comes from the idea of J. B. Say and James Mill, discussed in the text, that the act of supplying a good involves the intent to use the proceeds to purchase another good. As shall be explained, the charge that Malthus's system violates the law of markets is correct, but it is not a "logical" flaw, and Malthus's ideas are none the worse for it.

40 Hollander, Samuel (1992) *Classical Economics,* Toronto: University of Toronto Press, p. 252. For the view that Keynes derived his idea of aggregate demand theory from Malthus, see Kates, Steven (1994) The Malthusian origins of the General Theory: or How Keynes Came to Write a Book about Say's Law and Effective Demand. *History of Economics Review*, 21, pp. 10–20.

41 The referenced aspect is Malthus's rejection of the non-satiation principle, which is discussed in Chapters 2 and 3.

42 It is somewhat puzzling why Malthus states that landlord and capitalist consumption is diminished "by supposition." At least with regard to normally high-spending landlords, however, Malthus explains why their consumption diminishes when workers shift out of their employ—as unproductive labor—into manufacturing: "if no menial servants could be kept to take care of houses, furniture, carriages, horses, &c. it is quite clear that the demand for material luxuries and conveniences would vey soon abate, and the owners of land and capital would have very slender motives to employ them in the most productive manner." It is less clear to what the reference to capitalists—whom he assumes already consume little of their income—reducing their consumption refers. It could either mean that capitalists lose servants to manufacturing as do landlords—and reduce their consumption yet further—or it could mean that Malthus envisions that capitalists pour every available resource into capital investment during an investment boom, either as a precipitating cause of the boom, or as a reaction to the exuberance initially engendered by the boom. Malthus, p. 316.

43 Malthus, p. 236.

44 Malthus, p. 330. I interpret this passage, in conjunction with the following passage: "Almost all merchants and manufacturers save, in prosperous times, much more rapidly than it would be possible for the national capital to increase, so as to keep up the value of the produce," to mean that capitalists continue to save (and not consume) even after profits on new capital investment have become negative, but they do not continue to invest in new manufacturing. Therefore, their only alternative is to invest their ongoing profits (earned from sunk plant investment) and their prior accumulated savings (held as money or financial claims), into money and financial claims (private loans,

DOI: 10.1057/9781137562210.0005

government bonds etc...). This assertion is controversial. There is a popular conception that Malthus believes that capitalists invest all of their savings in production and do not hoard money or make loans. This is a matter—not the only one—where Malthus takes on opposing positions. In support of my position that saving can be held as money, he writes: "A circulating medium is absolutely necessary to any considerable saving; and even the manufacturers would get on but slowly, if he were obliged to accumulate in kind all the wages of his workmen... the circulating medium bears so important a part in the distribution of wealth, and the encouragement of industry, that it is hardly ever safe to set it aside in our reasonings..." In opposition, he writes "No political economist of the present day can by saving mean mere hoarding"; Malthus, p. 324n (first quote) and pp. 38–39 (second quote). Lionel Robbins, who was an influential proponent of the popular conception, acknowledges (actually "warns") that the question of whether Malthus believes that all saving is planned to be invested is a "controversial" matter, that is open to conflicting interpretation. See Robbins, Lionel (1998) *A History of Economic Thought: The LSE Lectures*. Princeton, NJ: Princeton University Press, p. 204. Even if the popular conception is correct, it does not alter the outcome of the process described in the text; the overproduction of goods leads to deflation, contraction in output, and layoffs.

45 In addition, Malthus questions whether wealthy landlords can be relied upon to consume a high proportion of their income. He expresses concern over the concentration of land ownership (though he finds reasons to resist calling for land reform in the England of his day). He writes; "Practically it had always been found that excessive wealth of the few is in no respect equivalent, with regard to effectual demand, to the more moderate wealth of the many." Malthus, *Principles of Political Economy*, p. 375.

46 See definition of Accumulation in Chapter 3.

47 Malthus, *Principles of Political Economy*, pp. 399–400.

48 The proposals made by Malthus involve increasing the income share earned by high-spending landlords at the expense of workers. He justifies the idea by arguing that workers will benefit from the increase in the overall size of the pie.

49 Ricardo, David (1951) *Works and Correspondence*, ed. P. Sraffa, vols. I–IX, IX, p. 16. In a letter dated July 21, 1821 to Malthus, Ricardo emphasizes the point that flexible wages, which he *assumes* must obtain, will ensure a speedy return to full employment.

> "You say, 'We know from repeated experience that the money price of labour never falls till many workmen have been for some time out of work.' I know no such thing; and, if wages were previously high, I can see no reason whatever why they should not fall before many labourers are thrown out of work. All general reasoning, I apprehend, is in favour of my view of this question, for why should some agree to go without any wages while others

DOI: 10.1057/9781137562210.0005

were most liberally rewarded? Once more I must say that a sudden and diminished demand for labour in this case must mean a diminished reward to the labourer, and not a diminished employment of him; he will work at least as much as before, but will have a less proportion of the produce of his work, and this will be so in order that his employer may have an adequate motive for employing him at all, which he certainly would not have if his share of the produce were reduced so low as to make increased production an evil rather than a benefit to him." Ricardo, *Works and Correspondence*, pp. 25–26.

50 Malthus might also argue that, even if wages rose, worker consumption may not rise appreciably if the new wage was above the level necessary to provide for necessaries. This is consistent with Malthus's belief that workers prefer indolence over working to earn money to purchase luxuries, which implies that the labor supply curve is backward bending. A backward bending labor supply curve could cause employment—and output—to fall in response to a rise in wages.

51 In his response to Malthus, Ricardo assumes that workers spend most of their wages on consumption.

52 Ricardo, *Works and Correspondence*, p. 16. This passage is almost identical to the passage quoted from Malthus on page 25. A crucial difference, however, is that Malthus refers to "converting revenue into capital' where as Ricardo refers to "[the] motive for accumulation." Where Malthus and Ricardo differ is in what each assumes capitalists will do with their savings when profit and risk on capital investment becomes too low to justify further investment. I have argued above that Malthus's writings imply that they will invest in money and financial claims, whereas I infer (partly based on the quote on page 28, but also on his belief that demand for goods is insatiable) that Ricardo believes capitalists will increase their consumption. Note that this passage implies that capitalists continue to have savings out of which either to consume or invest even as profits on new capital investment become negative. Capitalists must either continue to earn profits from sunk investment (including inventories), or hold money and financial claims, or some combination of all of them.

53 For the present purpose, I am neglecting the other sources of deficient demand cited by Malthus.

54 Here are two examples: "Modern interpreters have overlooked the blind persistence with which the Ricardians translated others' dynamics into comparative statics terms, and have assumed that the general glut controversy was a controversy over permanent secular stagnation rather than cyclical fluctuations." Sowell, *Classical Economics Reconsidered*, Princeton NJ: Princeton University Press, p. 46. "Time after time in these letters Malthus is talking plain sense, the force of which Ricardo, with his head in the clouds wholly fails to comprehend." Keynes, J. M. (1933) *Essays in Biography*, New York: WW Norton & Company (Reprint 1963), p. 123.

DOI: 10.1057/9781137562210.0005

55 Ricardo, *Works and Correspondence*, vols. I–IX, VII, p. 120. A comment by Malthus on general glut has also contributed to the mis-perception that he was exclusively focused on short-term dynamics: "... the question of a glut is exclusively whether it may be general, as well as particular, and not whether it may be permanent as well as temporary." Malthus, Thomas R. (1827) *Definitions in Political Economy*. London: John Murray, p. 62. This passage is quoted by Thomas Sowell in support of his conclusion that Malthus believes general glut to be a short-term phenomena. See Sowell, *Classical Economics Reconsidered*, pp. 46–47.

56 Samuel Hollander comprehensively refutes the widespread notion that Ricardo was unconcerned with short-term dynamics. See Hollander, *Classical Economics*, pp. 334–335.

57 Say, J. B. (1814) *Traité d'économie politique, second edition*, reprinted in 1944, Paris: Guillaumin, p. 145n.

58 Say, J. B. (1821) *Letters to Mr. Malthus on Several Subjects of Political Economy and on the Cause of Stagnation of commerce*. Reprint by August M. Kelly, New York (1967), p. 11.

59 Ibid., p. 27.

60 For a brief enumeration of the various ways Say's Law has been interpreted by economists, see Sowell, pp. 39–40, or Baumol, William (1999) Retrospectives: Say's Law. *The Journal of Economic Perspectives*, 13(1), pp. 195–204.

61 Ricardo, *Works and Correspondence*, vols. I–IX, I, p. 290.

62 Equilibrium in a market for good is the condition where the amount supplied equals the amount demanded for that good at the prevailing price in the market. Equilibrium for the economy as a whole—called general equilibrium—is the condition where every market for every good is in equilibrium.

63 Say, *Letters to Mr. Malthus on Several Subjects of Political Economy and on the Cause of Stagnation of commerce*, p. 3.

64 Ibid., p. 48.

65 Ibid. See pp. 48 and 51.

66 Technically, this means that the capitalist has violated his budget constraint by committing to spend more than he can possibly earn. The result is either a depletion of prior accumulated saving or repudiation of debts through debt restructuring or bankruptcy.

67 Ricardo, *Works and Correspondence*, vols. I–IX, VIII, p. 277.

68 Ibid., vols. I–IX, VIII, pp. 227–228.

69 Ibid., vols. I–IX, I, p. 293. Malthus responds directly to Ricardo's point. "Adam Smith has observed 'that he desire of food is limited in every man by the narrow capacity of the human stomach; but the desire of the conveniences and ornaments of building, dress, equipage, and household furniture, seems to have

DOI: 10.1057/9781137562210.0005

no limit or certain boundary.' ... that it has no limit must be allowed to be too strong an expression when we consider how it will be practically limited by the countervailing luxury of indolence, or by the general desire of mankind to better their condition, and make a provision for a family; a principle which, as Adam Smith himself states, is on the whole stronger than the principle which prompts to expense." Malthus, *Principles of Political Economy*, pp. 401–402.

70 Ricardo, *Works and Correspondence*, vols. I–IX, I, p. 296.

71 Ibid., p. 293.

72 Ibid., p. 293.

73 Malthus, *Principles of Political Economy*, p. 319.

74 Ibid., p. 322.

75 Ibid., pp. 324–345.

76 Ricardo, *Works and Correspondence*, vols. I–IX, VII, pp. 122–123.

77 Ibid., p. 67.

78 Malthus's premonition of liquidity trap, is not recognized by Keynes, in spite of his acknowledgment of Malthus as an inspiration and a precursor to his effective demand theory. Keynes apparently is not aware that Malthus had an embryonic theory of interest rates that is quite similar to his own.

79 Ricardo, *Works and Correspondence*, vols. I–IX, VIII, p. 260.

80 Say, *Letters to Mr. Malthus on Several Subjects of Political Economy and on the Cause of Stagnation of commerce*, p. 49n.

DOI: 10.1057/9781137562210.0005

2

Say's Principle and the Possibility of Deficient Demand

Abstract: *Malthus and Ricardo disagree over whether capitalists chronically consume less than they earn, which leads them to radically different conclusions about the nature of short term economic cycles and the possibility of secular stagnation. In this chapter the competing positions are placed into a general equilibrium framework, where it is shown that their respective conclusions hold up. If, as Ricardo contends, people are never satiated and ultimately spend all their income on final goods, it is plausible the economy hones in on full employment. If, as Malthus contends, capitalists spend only a small portion of their profits on final goods, the economy will not reach full employment, and output will fluctuate around a low growth trend that is determined by aggregate demand.*

Keywords: effective demand; general glut; Keynes and the classics; liquidity preference; Say's Principle

Aronoff, Daniel. *A Theory of Accumulation and Secular Stagnation: A Malthusian Approach to Understanding a Contemporary Malaise.* New York: Palgrave Macmillan, 2015. DOI: 10.1057/9781137562210.0006.

 DOI: 10.1057/9781137562210.0006

> The world is too much with us; late and soon,
> Getting and spending, we lay waste our powers;—
> Little we see in Nature that is ours;
> We have given our hearts away, a sordid boon.
>
> —William Wordsworth[1]

> All theories founded upon the assumption that mankind always produce and consume as much as they have the power to produce and consume, are founded upon a want of knowledge of the human character and of the motives by which it is usually influenced.
>
> —Thomas Malthus[2]

1 Say's Principle

The debate between Malthus, on one side, and Say and Ricardo, on the other side, over the possibility of general glut and secular stagnation, can be evaluated with more rigor than they were able to express, by using the algebraic formulation later developed by Leon Walras to describe the relationships between prices, transactions, and plans in a market economy.[3]

The basic idea stems from the budget constraint faced by all firms and households. In a simple formulation the agent lives for one period—born at zero and dies at "t"—and is endowed at the beginning of the period with a certain amount of money and other financial assets, called wealth (Wo). He can plan to spend his wealth on—say two—non-financial commodities or services, called goods, X and Y, in quantities dx and dy, which are sold at given prices Px and Py, and he can plan to retain a portion of his wealth, Wt. At the beginning of the period, before trading occurs, the agent formulates a plan of the purchases and sales he intends to carry out. His plan is predicated on the assumption that he is able carry out all trades he desires at the given prices. The requirement that agents formulate such a plan before executing trades is the only behavioral constraint this analysis requires. The quantity of each good or wealth asset he plans to purchase or sell is called his "notional" demand or supply for that item. He may, or may not realize his plan. It depends upon whether there are counterparties who are willing and able to trade with him in the quantities he desires at the given prices. The amount he is able to actually offer to purchase or sell a given good—when he

DOI: 10.1057/9781137562210.0006

executes his trades in the marketplace—is his "effective demand" or "effective supply" of that item.[4] If, for example, he is unable to carry out all of his planned transactions, his effective demand for a particular item may be below his notional demand for that item. This can occur if the proceeds he is able to generate from sales of other items turns out below the quantities he had planned for. His realized purchases and sales at the given market prices may therefore diverge from what he initially planned for. The budget constraint of the agent, assuming unrestricted ability to trade at given prices, is expressed by:

$$Pxdx + Pydy - (Wo - Wt) \equiv 0 \qquad (2.1)$$

Identity (2.1) states that a person must plan to allocate all that he owns among goods (which he can consume or hold) and financial assets.[5] The agent has no choice but to do so, since his stuff has to end up somewhere and, by assumption, (2.1) includes everything he owns. Equation (2.1) is an identity because it applies no matter what is the behavioral motivation of the agent. Economists Robert Clower and Axel Leijonhufvud have called it "Say's Principle," which they define as the assumption that "the net value of an individual's planned trades is identically zero."[6] If, however, the additional behavioral assumption is made that a person will spend all of his wealth on goods, *identity* (2.1) becomes *equation* (2.2):

$$Pxdx + Pydy = Wo \qquad (2.2)$$

Equation (2.2) is not an identity because it imposes a limitation on choices the agent makes, while still respecting his budget constraint. It implies that the agent will not plan to hold money or financial assets when he dies. There is no necessity that he makes this choice. It reflects the assumption that there is always some good a person will want, no matter how many goods he already has. This is the non-satiation principle, which is a behavioral assumption that is not implied by Say's Principle. Malthus does not believe that capitalists behave in accordance with the non-satiation principle. According to him, capitalists produce goods in order to accumulate wealth, not to acquire other goods. Nor does he believe that high-wage workers obey the precept, since they lack a desire for luxuries. Notice, however, that there is nothing in Malthus's conjecture that places it in opposition to Say's Principle. Ricardo on the other hand—like almost all

DOI: 10.1057/9781137562210.0006

economists after him—posits that people behave in accordance with the non-satiation principle: "I consider the wants and tastes of mankind as unlimited."[7]

The example can easily be extended in two ways that make it more realistic. One is to add the number of goods, including labor, which the person may acquire or sell. Now there are a finite number of goods indexed by $n \in \{1,\ldots,n,\ldots,N]$, with prices of $Pn \in \{P1,\ldots,Pn,\ldots PN-1, 1\}$, where the Nth good is money and its price = 1 (since all other prices are quoted in terms of money). We are still in an artificial world of the present, and the agent may begin the period with endowments of some goods $Wn \in \{W1,\ldots,Wn,\ldots,WN\}$. For each good the agent will decide how much he plans to hold (or consume) at the end of the period (dn – Wn), which represents the agent's excess notional demand for the nth good.[8] If he desires to purchase more of the good than he is initially endowed with, his excess notional demand will be positive. If he desires to sell off a portion of his endowment in order to purchase other goods, his excess notional demand will be negative (also called "excess notional supply"). The excess notional demand is denoted as Xn. The budget constraint of the agent, assuming unrestricted ability to trade at given prices, is now expressed as the identity:

$$P1X1 + \cdots + PnXn + \cdots + XN \equiv 0 \qquad (2.3)$$

There are two important things to note about identity (2.3). One is that the budget constraint still sums to zero. This reflects that the agent must allocate all that he owns somewhere. The second thing to note is that (2.3) applies to planned trades at given prices, and the agent may not be able to carry out his planned trades.

The analysis can be extended to include a finite number of other agents, who are indexed by adding a second subscript $k \in \{1,\ldots,k,\ldots,K\}$. Agent k is denoted as Ak, and his excess demand for good Xn is denoted as Xnk. The nature of the items subject to trade can be partitioned along the lines that are similar—though not perfectly matched—to the way Malthus and Ricardo divided them. "Final goods" are the objects of consumer demand, which includes food, clothes, luxuries, and inventories;[9] "wealth" includes fixed capital (which includes land), circulating capital, financial claims,[10] and money; and labor refers to workers who are paid wages—"w." The system of transactions among all K agents is depicted in Table 2.1.[11]

DOI: 10.1057/9781137562210.0006

TABLE 2.1 *Aggregate budget matrix for an economy*

Agents	Final goods and labor							Wealth			
				Food	Clothing	Labor		Fixed and circulating capital	Financial claims	Money	Net value
(Ak)	X_1	X_2		X_{n-2}	X_{n-1}	X_n		X_{N-2}	X_{N-1}	X_N	
A_1	$P_1X_{1,1}+$	$P_2X_{2,1}+$	……..+	$P_{n-2}X_{n-2,1}+$	$P_{n-1},X_{n-1,1}+$	$wX_{n,1}+$	……..+	$P_{N-2}X_{N-2,1}+$	$P_{N-1}X_{N-1,1}+$	$X_{N,1}\equiv$	0
A_2	$P_1X_{1,2}+$	$P_2X_{2,2}+$	……..+	$P_{n-2}X_{n-2,2}+$	$P_{n-1},X_{n-1,2}+$	$wX_{n,2}+$	……..+	$P_{N-2}X_{N-2,2}+$	$P_{N-1}X_{N-1,2}+$	$X_{N,2}\equiv$	0
⋮											
AK	$P_1X_{1,K}+$	$P_2X_{2,K}+$	……..+	$P_{n-2}X_{n-2,k}+$	$P_{n-1},X_{n-1,2}+$	$wX_{n,K}+$	……..+	$P_{N-2}X_{N-2,k}+$	$P_{N-1}X_{N-1,K}+$	$X_{N,K}\equiv$	0
Aggregate excess demands	P_1X_1+	P_2X_2+	……..+	$P_{n-2}X_{n-2}+$	$P_{n-1},X_{n-1}+$	wX_n+	……..+	$P_{N-2}X_{N-2}+$	$P_{N-1}X_{N-1}+$	$X_N\equiv$	0

DOI: 10.1057/9781137562210.0006

There are four features of Table 2.1 that are important for the present analysis. One is that the sum of aggregate excess notional demands for all goods and assets is zero, which obtains because the aggregate of excess notional demands is simply the sum of the sums of all individual budget equations, each of which is zero by definition. This demonstrates that Say's Principle holds for the economy as a whole. The second feature is that the excess aggregate notional demand in any particular good need not equal zero. Say's Principle does not imply that all markets clear (i.e. planned purchases equal planned sales at given prices). This point is underscored by the observation that the matrix describes planned trades that obtain for any non-negative combination of prices, not just combinations of prices at which excess notional demand is zero in each market. The third feature is that there can be an aggregate excess notional demand for wealth, which implies a negative excess notional demand (or excess supply) for final goods and labor. The fourth feature is that the table applies to notional demands. Actual trades involve matching buyers and sellers, therefore if notional excess demands are not zero at initial prices established in the market, the volume of goods traded, and possibly the prices at which they are traded, will have to change. If prices do not change, or if price changes do not clear markets (i.e. if some excess demands are non-zero), an agent who cannot sell all of the goods he planned, will have to curtail his purchases. For example, a person who becomes unemployed (i.e. cannot sell his planned labor services), will suffer a loss of labor income (wXk) and will have to reduce his purchases below plan by that amount (i.e. his effective demand is below his notional demand).

It is possible to describe the behavior of the three social classes in the context of Table 2.1.[12] Landlords collect rents that are derived from the sale of food. They spend their income as necessary on circulating capital required to cultivate and maintain their land. The rest, according to Malthus, they spend on servants—by employing labor—and final goods.[13] Workers derive their income from the sale of their labor services for wages and—to the extent they earn low wages—spend it all on final goods. Capitalists derive their income from sales of final goods and spend it on wages, capital, and financial assets.

Finally, the analysis can be brought one step closer to reality by including a time dimension. This can be done by adding a second subscript $t \in \{1,\ldots,t,\ldots,\infty\}$ to each good, which represents the date

DOI: 10.1057/9781137562210.0006

of delivery of that good; Xnt. The kth agent's intertemporal budget identity becomes:

$$\sum_{i=0}^{N} \sum_{t=0}^{\infty} PntXntk \equiv 0 \tag{2.4}$$

The introduction of time does not alter the analysis in any way. It can be assumed that agents live forever (not very realistic), or that there are overlapping generations, where parents have altruistic feelings for their children (somewhat more realistic), so that family dynasties behave like infinitely lived agents.

2 General glut, secular stagnation, Accumulation, and non-satiation

The concept of general glut involves an excess supply of every final good. Say's Principle implies there cannot be a notional—or planned—general glut when considering all traded items, since aggregate excess notional demands sum to zero. If, however, the analysis is restricted to final goods, this result no longer holds. Say's Principle does not imply that aggregate excess notional demands for any subset of goods will sum to zero.[14] However, if the non-satiation principle applies, which means that everyone desires to spend all their resources on final goods, and invest nothing in wealth (other than profit generating capital investment, in which case the excess demand for capital is zero—see below), then a general glut can only occur if the labor market does not clear and there is an excess notional supply of labor. This explains why economists devote so much attention on the labor market.

Even if the sum of aggregate notional excess demands for final goods are zero, the possibility that actual supply can exceed effective demand for each final good at prevailing market prices cannot be ruled out, because sellers may misjudge demand. As Ricardo states, "men err in their productions." Yet, when this occurs, Ricardo reasonably conjectures that "there may not be adequate motives for production, and therefore things will not be produced," which will cause the glut to dissipate. If, by contrast, the non-satiation principle does not hold and there is an excess notional demand for wealth, Say's Principle implies that there is also an excess notional supply of final goods and labor, which can be seen in identity (2.5):

DOI: 10.1057/9781137562210.0006

Sum of excess notional demands for final goods and labor + Sum of excess notional demands for wealth ≡ 0 (2.5)

Rearranging the terms in (2.5) yields identity (2.6), which says that the excess notional demands for wealth must always be matched by an equal excess notional supplies of final goods and labor.

Sum of notional excess demands for wealth ≡ Sum of notional excess supplies of final goods and labor (2.6)

Note that an increase in capital investment that is motivated by an expectation of future profit does not imply a deficiency in aggregate demand for final goods (notional or effective). This can occur if there is a demand from final goods manufacturers to purchase products produced by intermediate goods manufacturers. A textile mill, for instance, may wish to expand its facilities. In Malthus's framework, if the workers who are drawn to manufacturing from unproductive employment are engaged in producing capital goods, the supply of final goods will be unchanged, and since labor employment is not increased, so will the demand for final goods be unchanged. There will be no general glut (notional or effective).

Capital investment may be made for a time to ramp up potential output to a higher level by improving labor productivity, but only if capitalists perceive they can sell the increased future output and make a profit. Eventually—for a given state of technology—a steady state of per capita capital/labor ratio will be reached and net investment will stop. When population is growing, capitalists can profit by making capital investments to equip the growing increment of workers in future periods with the tools required to be productive. Therefore, there can be a positive rate of net investment when there is population growth without creating an aggregate excess supply of potential output. In these cases production is shifted from final goods to capital goods, and the net result is the maintenance or increase in output over time. Such activity is consistent with non-satiation.[15] Moreover, to the extent a capitalist accumulates capital goods as a store of wealth, he is employing unproductive labor and, from the standpoint of aggregate demand, it is no different than the work that servants perform for landlords.

Malthus and Ricardo both believe that capitalists make capital investments to generate profit, and that capital investment will discontinue if profits on new investment drop to a low level. They differ in their assumptions about how capitalists will spend their profits and accumulated wealth when capital investment has reached its maximum level. Ricardo appears to think that capitalists will increase their demand for final goods, while Malthus disagrees. The logical implication—though he does not state it explicitly—is that Malthus believes capitalists invest their excess profits in money and financial claims.[16]

It is at this point that the possibility of secular stagnation enters. If capitalists generate a significant excess notional demand for financial claims or money, they must also generate a matching excess notional supply of final goods. This conclusion follows from their budget constraint, given that they do not offer labor services and their excess demand for capital goods is, by assumption, zero. If their desire for wealth is unquenchable, and if the profit on the incremental investment is zero or negative, there will be no set of prices at which the excess supply of goods will be eliminated and in aggregate the realized transactions in goods will be below what sellers wish to sell. This chronic deficiency in demand is not curable by rebalancing the proportions of goods produced, as Say and Ricardo maintain. This violation of the non-satiation principle is the source of Malthus's concern over deficient demand and the tendency to general glut and secular stagnation.[17] As discussed in Chapter 1, Malthus and Ricardo understand the fundamental source of their divergence in opinion on economic matters to stem from the question of whether capitalists have an excess notional demand for wealth, and therefore fail to behave in accordance with the non-satiation principle.

3 Intuitive dynamics—the attraction to equilibrium

If the non-satiation principle applies, it follows that (a) there cannot be a persistent general glut because aggregate excess notional supply for final goods and labor is zero, and (b) any excess demand/supply for particular final goods and/or labor reflect a misalignment between the configuration of quantities and prices supplied and demanded. These correspond to two key points made by Ricardo and Say. Moreover, there is a plausible mechanism by which excess demand/supply will be eliminated and the economy directed toward equilibrium (i.e. zero excess demand for each final good and labor).[18] Sellers of final goods (or labor) experiencing positive excess demand will have an incentive to charge a higher price and buyers will have an incentive to offer a

DOI: 10.1057/9781137562210.0006

higher price. A price increase ought to deter some purchasers and attract suppliers. These adjustments will eliminate the excess demand. Conversely, there will be pressure for a price reduction for items experiencing excess supply, which will encourage some purchasers to buy more and cause some suppliers to discontinue production. These adjustments will tend to eliminate the excess supply. A reduction in excess supplies and demands for individual final goods and labor moves the economy toward equilibrium, which accords with Ricardo's view that the economy hones in on equilibrium.

This result does not hold where the non-satiation principle does not obtain. If some people—such as Malthus's capitalists—desire to accumulate wealth, there may be an incurable excess demand for wealth. If there is an aggregate notional excess demand for financial claims and money, it follows from Say's Principle that there must be a corresponding aggregate notional excess supply of final goods and labor, which cannot be eliminated by adjustments in the prices of any items or combinations of individual items.[19] The absence of non-satiation (more precisely, an incurable excess demand for wealth) implies that there will be sellers of final goods or labor who cannot find buyers at any prices. It also means that, without more information on institutional features of the economy, it is not possible to predict the path by which the economy will evolve.[20] Therefore, criticism of Malthus based on the lack of structure to his model is misplaced. If he is right about capitalists saving behavior, the economy will evolve in a chaotic fashion and it will not hone in on full employment. It is not reasonable to judge Malthus's model by standards that are suitable for equilibrium analysis.

4 Wage flexibility and full employment

The analysis above enables an evaluation of the debate between Malthus and Ricardo over whether wage and consumption flexibility will cause the economy to return to full employment when it has deviated. Ricardo maintains that wage and capitalist consumption adjustments can, and will, ensure that the economy hones in on full employment equilibrium. Malthus denies that there is any mechanism that can be relied upon to steer the economy toward full employment. Figure 2.1 depicts the relationship between aggregate final goods output and the labor market. For any level of manufactured final goods output (Y)—shown on the vertical

DOI: 10.1057/9781137562210.0006

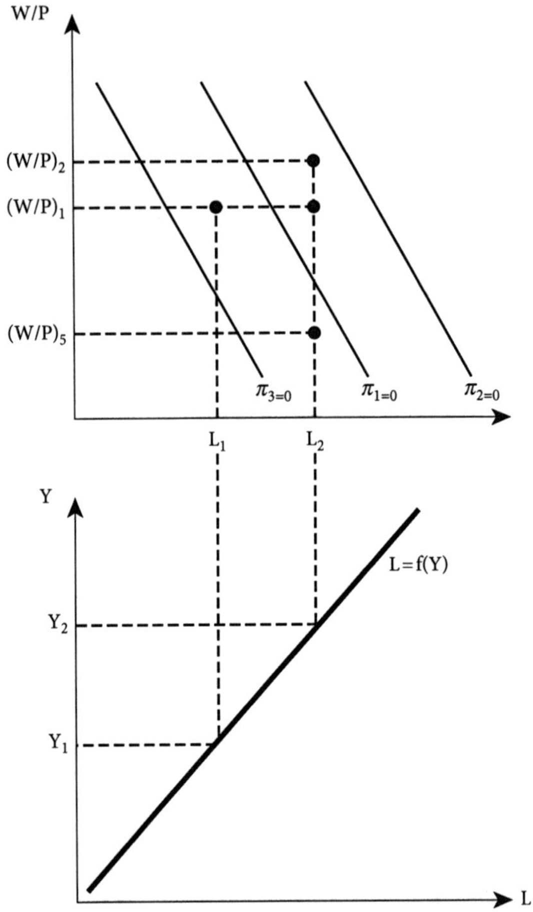

FIGURE 2.1 *The relation of output, employment, real wages, and profit for the economy described by Malthus and Ricardo*

axis of the lower panel—the production function L = F(Y) relates the volume of labor required to produce it, which is displayed on the horizontal axis. The upper panel displays the volume of labor supplied, and the maximum volume that can be employed at any real wage rate, (w/p), where “w” is the nominal wage[21] and “p” is an index of the price level of manufactured goods. Labor supply is increasing in (w/p), which reflects that higher wages will induce more people to work.[22] The downward

DOI: 10.1057/9781137562210.0006

sloping curve labeled ($\pi 1 = 0$) is the schedule of real wages at which profits are zero for the initial output level Y1. Actual real wages will be below the zero profit curves, which reflects that capitalists will not produce if it is unprofitable to do so.

We now examine the boom and bust phase of the cycle described by Malthus. In the boom phase, when workers are drawn out of unproductive labor into manufacturing final goods, Malthus argues that the increase in manufactured final goods output will outstrip demand, since aggregate demand does not increase. This result from the confluence of three assumptions: (1) wages do not increase, (2) capitalists do not spend profits on consumption, and (3) capitalists will not continue to produce what they cannot profitably sell. In Figure 2.1 the boom is reflected in the increase in manufacturing output from Y1 to Y2. In order to support the increased output, manufacturing employment must increase, from L1 to L2. The conflict this gives rise to can be seen in the upper panel, where the maximum volume of labor that can be profitably employed at the initial real wage of (w/p)1 is below the volume necessary to produce output of Y2. The reason is that, according to Malthus, demand has not risen (recall that total employment has not increased, rather there has been a shift in employment from the unproductive sector to manufacturing), so the zero profit line remains at $\pi 1$.[23]

The fundamental problem stems from the fact that capitalists do not increase their consumption when their profits increase. This can be demonstrated be examining budget equation of the capitalist. Define "X" as the capital good (or an index of capital goods, including wages) and "C" as the manufactured final good (or an index of manufactured consumer goods). The price of a unit of X is Px and the price of a unit of C is Pc. The budget equation of the kth capitalist can be expressed as the sum of profits (which are assumed to be positive): $\pi = (PcCt(ks) - PxXtk)$, where "Ct(ks)" is the quantity of manufactured final goods sold in the market by the kth capitalist. The quantity of manufactured final goods consumed at by the kth capitalist is "Ct(kp)." Assume there is no population growth and that capital per capita is at its stationary level (so that the only capital expenditure is for repair and replacement of depreciated items). Finally, we reflect Malthus's behavioral assumption that "The great object of [capitalists] lives is to save a fortune...." These assumptions yield inequality (2.7).

$$PcCt(kp) - (PctCt(ks) - PxtXtk) < 0 \tag{2.7}$$

DOI: 10.1057/9781137562210.0006

Rearranging terms and substituting "profits" and "consumption" for the terms in equation (2.7) yields:

$$\text{Capitalist consumption} < \text{Capitalist profit} \tag{2.8}$$

inequalities (2.7) and (2.8) reflect that, for the subsystem of production and distribution of final goods, the law of markets does not hold; capitalists plan to sell more than they plan to purchase. The reason they plan to sell more than they purchase is that they desire to retain a portion of their profit and not spend it (i.e., to accumulate it).

Another drag on demand arises from unemployed workers. After the initial expansion to Y2 output is pulled back, workers are laid off, and if they do not immediately find employment in the unproductive sector, expenditure is below the level that obtained at the beginning. This causes the zero profit line to shift leftward to $\pi 3$, which is beneath the initial zero profit line $\pi 1$. It is easy to imagine how this could trigger a multiplier process of declining employment, although Malthus does not draw this conclusion.

Ricardo argues that wages are likely to increase as a result of the bidding that manufacturers will have to undertake to entice workers into their employ. If workers spend all of their wages on final goods (i.e. they obey the non-satiation principle), then an increase in wages from (w/p)1 to (w/p)2, as output increases from Y1 to Y2, will increase demand and shift the zero profit to the right, to $\pi 2$. Ricardo is correct that a higher wage can induce higher employment. It depends on the impact of a wage increase on profits; if the effect is strong enough, employment will increase. If capitalists spent a portion of their increased profits on final goods—as Ricardo contends they will—the zero profit line would shift even further to the right. Therefore, this analysis shows that Malthus and Ricardo were correct in believing that the question of whether a general glut can be avoided when capitalists' ramp up production centers on whether or not capitalists are intent upon accumulating wealth and whether wages are flexible.

In the bust phase, when unemployment is high, Malthus does not point to any market adjustment that will restore full employment. Rather, he argues that the bust phase is the normal state of an economy plagued by underconsumption. Occasionally, the capitalist drive to accumulate wealth enabled by prior accumulation and encouraged by a spike in demand, fuels a boom in production and a general glut. But

DOI: 10.1057/9781137562210.0006

after inventories pile up due to insufficient demand, capitalists contract production and the economy settles back into a state of resource underutilization.

Ricardo claims that, when unemployment is high, a wage reduction can restore full employment, since the zero profit line is downward sloped. In Figure 2.1, if the initial wage is (w/p)1 and the zero profit line has shifted down to π3, a reduction in wage to (w/p)3 will cause employment to increase, since the shift in wage lowers cost but does not affect demand, so long as capitalists spend all their increased profits on final goods. His advice makes sense where the non-satiation principle obtains. As in the case of the boom, the point of dispute between Malthus and Ricardo over whether a market economy will spontaneously hone in on full employment, revolves around the question of whether or not wages are flexible and whether or not the non-satiation principle obtains.

5 The outcome of the Malthus–Ricardo debate

Ricardo was (and is) perceived by the majority of economists as the hands down winner of the debate over general glut and secular stagnation. Keynes writes of

> the almost total obliteration of Malthus' line of approach and the complete domination of Ricardo's for a period of a hundred years.[24]
>
> Ricardo conquered England as completely as the Holy Inquisition conquered Spain. Not only was his theory accepted by the city, by statesmen and by the academic world. But controversy ceased; the other point of view completely disappeared; it ceased to be discussed.[25]

Ricardo won on both the substantive and methodological levels. Most economists—during that time as after—recognize that a general glut or a deficiency in demand for labor and final goods violates the law of markets, but many economists draw the incorrect conclusion that a model or approach that violates the law of markets cannot be logically constructed. When Malthus argues that a desire to accumulate causes a deficiency in demand for final goods or labor, he is on solid logical ground. According to Say's Principle, there is no other possible outcome. So, the real question is not whether Malthus's theory violates the law of markets, but whether there is a desire to accumulate by an economically significant group.

DOI: 10.1057/9781137562210.0006

What occurred in the development of economic doctrine is that the principle of non-satiation, which Malthus and Ricardo treat as a potentially falsifiable empirical proposition, has been incorporated as an axiom of economic theory. It is embodied in Lionel Robbins's canonical definition of economics as "the science which studies human behavior as a relationship between ends and scarce means which have alternative uses."[26] The "means" Robbins is referring to are possibilities for producing final goods; and they can only be scarce if "ends" (i.e. wants) are not satiated. The entire corpus of economic theory relies upon non-satiation. The combined assumptions of non-satiation and declining marginal utility—alongside other restrictions on functional forms—allow economic behavior to be modeled as a maximization exercise. Nobel Laurate economist Gary Becker described the theoretical core of economics as "the combined assumptions of maximizing behavior, market equilibrium and stable preferences, used relentlessly and unflinchingly."[27] If, among the objectives to be maximized is wealth, then the concept encompasses Accumulation to some extent (but not to the extent that the desire for wealth relative to final goods does not diminish as its quantity increases).[28] In virtually all applications, however, the object of maximization is a final good, not money or wealth.

The recent advent of behavioral economics, which is devoted to incorporating more realistic representations of human decision-making into economic theory, is no less committed to the axiom of maximizing (or, equivalently, "optimizing") behavior. Matthew Rabin, a leading behavioral economist describes the research program as exploring "the potential for using neoclassical (broadly defined) optimization models to integrate insights from psychology on the limits to rationality into economics... [since] many human limits to full rationality are, in fact, well understood in terms of optimization."[29] However, since it is in the nature of the behavioral approach to consider motivations that extend beyond the traditional paradigm, perhaps it will become the avenue through which Accumulation will be considered as a behavioral feature that shapes the optimization exercise for certain people.

Another dimension in which Ricardo prevailed over Malthus is that economics has developed as an equilibrium theory—a state where all plans are mutually consistent. Even where the description is dynamic, as with the dynamic stochastic general equilibrium technique that underpins modern macroeconomics, what is described is a system that is

DOI: 10.1057/9781137562210.0006

always in equilibrium. There are sound reasons for this. There have been attempts to develop an approach to disequilibrium behavior, but none of the efforts have yet come to fruition. Yet, the economy may nevertheless spend considerable time outside of an equilibrium state and, as argued by Malthus, it may not always hone in on equilibrium. There is a need to come to grips with these situations.

Malthus does not specify any particular outcome or time-path for economic variables. His idea of Accumulation establishes no more than a boundary delimiting a space—a rather large space—within which economic outcomes can occur. One line of criticism of Malthus's ideas is that they are not sufficiently precise to allow economists to use them as a foundation for constructing mathematical models linking individual behavior to economic outcomes. The standard economic approach is to apply axioms of individual decision-making to a particular environment to deduce economic outcomes. However, Malthus describes dynamic processes that take place outside of equilibrium,[30] where plans are not mutually compatible and where there are multiple channels of causation at work. The fact that Malthus's ideas do not fit the mold of the standard paradigm does not mean they are incoherent. In fact, the limitations that economists have encountered in using the standard approach should lead them to consider alternative approaches. Economist John Sutton has written:

> Much of the difficulty economists have encountered over the past fifty years can be traced to the fact that the economic environments we seek to model are sometimes too messy to be fitted into the mold of a well-behaved complete model of the standard kind.[31]

6 Keynes and Malthus

Keynes famously (or infamously) claims Malthus as an inspiration for his theory of aggregate demand and he fully recognizes the significance of Malthus's attempt to add aggregate demand into the corpus of economic theory.[32] There has been much controversy concerning the degree of influence Malthus had on Keynes and the affinity in their ideas.[33] Yet, whatever one thinks of the similarities and differenced between them, Keynes is surely right to place his theory of aggregate demand in the intellectual tradition of Malthus's earlier attempt to incorporate aggregate demand into economic theory. Fundamentally, they both endeavor to

DOI: 10.1057/9781137562210.0006

augment economics in a similar direction. However, like most scholars, Keynes finds Malthus's explanation of the effect of aggregate demand to lack coherence:

> Malthus, indeed had vehemently opposed Ricardo's doctrine that it was impossible for effective demand to be deficient; but vainly. For, since Malthus was unable to explain clearly (apart from an appeal to the facts of common observation) how and why effective demand could be deficient or excessive, he failed to furnish an alternative construction.[34]

In the first two chapters of this book I have argued to the contrary that Malthus provides a coherent explanation of "how and why effective demand could be deficient or excessive." Moreover, I contend that Keynes fails to recognize that the fundamental issue between Malthus and Ricardo is a difference of opinion over the existence of Accumulation as a motive in behavior. Keynes does not take up the issue of Accumulation, except to comment that an overconcentration of wealth—where some people spend less than they save—will not persist because it will drive down interest rates to a level that will force wealth-holders to spend their principal; a process he calls "the Euthanasia of the Rentier." He does identify excess notional saving (over investment) as the source of depressed demand. But he looks to the failure of prices—specifically interest rates—to adjust to clear markets, rather than an insatiable desire to accumulate wealth, as the cause of an excess of saving and, in consequence, a deficiency in aggregate demand.

Keynes maintains that there is more at stake than the fact that nominal interest rates cannot fall below zero. In his 1933 essay on Malthus, Keynes treats the idea that planned saving can exceed investment at zero interest rates as old hat: "Twenty years ago I should have retorted to Malthus that the state of affairs he envisages could not occur unless the rate of interest had first fallen to zero."[35] He believes that a much more pervasive source of dysfunction is caused by the desire people have to hold liquid money as a precaution against uncertainty. This "liquidity preference" implies that wealth-holders will require to earn a positive rate of interest—the more positive the greater is the perceived uncertainty—in order to hold bonds and other less liquid securities, instead of money. Liquidity preference creates a lower bound of interest rates—above zero—below which lending will not occur. This means that there will be investment projects with positive expected return, which are unable to obtain funding because their return lies beneath the lower bound. Thus, argues Keynes, in a

DOI: 10.1057/9781137562210.0006

world with unexploited potential profitable investment opportunities, there may yet be an excess of notional saving over investment, a situation which has become known as liquidity trap. In this way, liquidity preference creates the potential for a chronic deficiency of demand for final goods.

Keynes claims that his theory of liquidity preference is the key to a theory of aggregate demand and secular stagnation; that it provides the missing component in Malthus's conception. He interprets Malthus's allegedly unsupported conjecture about the importance of aggregate demand as a precursor to his own fully developed theory. This explains Keynes's remark that:

> Malthus defect lay in his overlooking entirely the part played by the rate of interest...Malthus perceived, as often, what was true; but it is essential to a complete comprehension of why it is true, to explain how an excess of frugality does not bring with it a decline to zero in the rate of interest.[36]

In asserting that his theory of interest is the missing piece of Malthus's explanation of the importance of aggregate demand, Keynes underestimates the fecundity of Malthus's ideas. First, he overlooks Malthus's challenge to the non-satiation principle and its implication for aggregate demand. Second, Keynes misses Malthus's anticipation of liquidity trap, as evidenced by his reference to "The fall in the interest on money and the difficulty of finding employment for capital."[37] Malthus recognizes that an excess of notional saving would cause interest rates to fall, but he does not specifically identify the fact that interest rates have a lower bound as the locus causes of deficient demand—as does Keynes. The reason is that Malthus does not think an adjustment of interest rates can cause notional saving and investment to become equal when capitalists are engaged in Accumulation. Keynes believes, as do most economists, that saving will decline and investment will rise as interest rates fall. By this reasoning, there is an interest rate—though it may lie beneath the lower bound of what can be achieved in the market—at which notional saving and investment can be brought into equality. Malthus, on the other hand, would argue that saving will increase as interest rates fall. This is so because a decline in borrowing costs implies an increase in profits—holding all else constant—which, according to Malthus, will be saved. An incurable excess demand for financial claims and money imply an excess supply of final goods and labor no matter what the configuration of prices and interest rates.

DOI: 10.1057/9781137562210.0006

In the years since the General Theory was published, the idea that deficient demand is caused by liquidity preference has been eclipsed by the idea that deficient demand is caused by sluggish wage and price adjustments in response to notional excess labor and goods supply. The proposition that those rigidities are important is what Keynesian economics has come to mean. Meanwhile, Malthus's notion that Accumulation can create chronic excess goods supply and short-term instability has remained dormant, except with are few non-mainstream economists, such as the neo-Marxists Paul Baran and Paul Sweezy and their acolytes, who have kept the flame alive into the late 20th century.[38] Part II of this book is an attempt to revive this tradition and to persuade the reader that the theory of Accumulation provides the most compelling account of the malaise the US economy has been experiencing over the past two decades.

Notes

1 The World is Too Much With Us (1806).

2 Malthus, Thomas R. (1836) *Principles of Political Economy*, reprinted by August M. Kelley, New York (1964), p. 424.

3 Leon Walras was a French economist who developed, among other innovations, the mathematical representation of a system of interconnected markets, known as general equilibrium theory, in the late 1800s.

4 Note that Walras does not consider situations where trades take place at "non-market clearing" prices (i.e. prices at which supply and demand for goods are not equal). Walras uses the metaphor of an auctioneer who calls out orders at different prices to determine the equilibrium prices before trading commences. If trading takes place at non-market clearing prices, or if the institutional structure of the market, or asymmetric information among agents, does not permit all willing seller and buyers to match up and trade at the given prices, then effective demand and supply may differ from notional demand and supply.

5 There are two subsidiary assumptions: (1) the agent can only enter into voluntary trades—he cannot confiscate or steal—and (2) the "law of one price" prevails so there is a single price for each good. The first assumption is enforced by morals and the law, the second assumption is enforced by competition.

6 Clower, Robert W. and Axel Leijonhufvud (Fall 1973) Say's Principle, What It Means and Doesn't Mean. *Intermountain Economic Review*. Reprinted in Leijonhufvud, Axel (1981) *Information and Coordination: Essays in Macroeconomic Theory*. New York: Oxford University Press, p. 80.

DOI: 10.1057/9781137562210.0006

7 Ricardo, David (1951) *Works and Correspondence*, ed. P. Sraffa, vols. I–IX, VI, pp. 134–135.

8 Note that the agent is endowed with labor power—the ability to work—which he can sell to employers in exchange for money, financial claims or goods.

9 The reason for including final goods inventories in the "final goods" sector is the assumption made by Malthus and Ricardo that all final goods are usually for sale (except in unusual instances where they may be held for speculation).

10 Financial claims include, inter alia, bank deposits, government debt, and private debt.

11 Note that Table 2.1 does not include a government sector. The government budget constraint would involve tax collection (which would subtract from agents resources), issuance of bonds (which would add to wealth at a point in time, but not ultimately, if it is assumed that the debt is repaid), and capital and final goods demand. While it is mandatory to include government when discussing its impact on the economy, it is not absolutely necessary that it be included for this exposition. Therefore, I have omitted consideration of government to simplify the analysis.

12 Note that Table 2.1 does not have a foreign trade sector. It is omitted to simplify the analysis. Its inclusion would not alter any of the results.

13 The saving behavior of very rich landlords is ignored.

14 Note this implies that the law of markets—which the proposition that the excess demands for all final goods are zero—is not a logical implication of decision problem faced by the agents in the economy. That is why, as stated in footnote 39, Chapter 1, the charge lodged against Malthus that his ideas violated the law of markets, while true, does not imply any error in Malthus's reasoning.

15 The modern neoclassical growth model, which is a workhorse in economic theory, requires both non-satiation and, in its basic version, the assumption that no individual would ever want to have positive wealth asymptotically. See Acemoglu, Daron (2014) Course Lectures on Economic Growth, Lectures 5 and 6 "Neoclassical Growth," available at http://economics.mit.edu/files/10231. I do not address either Malthus's or Ricardo's theory of capital accumulation and growth, which is significantly governed by their assumption that population increases whenever the wage rate is above subsistence and that the production of food from land is subject to declining marginal productivity. The interaction of these forces will cause wages to ultimately trend to subsistence and profits to trend to zero over time (as a result of a progressively higher food bill paid to landlords). This dismal prediction of long-run trend is the source of Thomas Carlyle's description of political economy: "Not a 'gay science,' I should say, like some we have heard of; no, a dreary, desolate and, indeed, quite abject and distressing one; what we

might call, by way of eminence, the dismal science." Carlyle, Thomas (1849). Occasional Discourse on the Negro Question. *Fraser's Magazine for Town and Country*, XL, p. 672. Happily, this prediction has never yet proven true!

16 There is a popular conception that Malthus believed that capitalists would continue plowing their profits and wealth into capital investment no matter what the rate of return. This opinion is contradicted by several passages from Malthus quoted in Chapter 1.

17 Malthus also cites the workers' lack of demand for luxuries (in the short term) as another source of stagnation. He might be correct that it will limit growth, but it is not a source of deficient demand. If workers lack a taste for luxuries as Malthus contends, they will not demand goods with the portion of their wages that are above the level necessary to provide for necessities. However, this does not necessarily generate an excess notional supply of goods. According to Malthus, their "indolence or love of ease" will cause many workers to reduce their labor supply, which will prevent labor income from exceeding worker's demand for goods. What Malthus describes is a backward bending labor supply curve, which implies that employment declines when wages rise beyond a certain level, because workers withdraw from employment. Therefore, while Malthus is correct to assert that "the effect of a preference of indolence to luxuries would evidently be to occasion a want of demand for the returns of the increased powers of production," he is wrong to conclude that the reduced demand leads capitalists to "throw laborers out of employment." On this last point, Malthus confuses a movement along the labor supply curve as wages rise, with an inward shift of the labor demand curve. See Malthus, pp. 320–321.

18 It needs to be noted that the requirements for a general equilibrium to exist are unrealistically restrictive. The concept of equilibrium is a heuristic that is rarely achieved even for an individual good. For a rigorous analysis of equilibrium, see Debreu, Gerard (1959) *Theory of Value: An Axiomatic Analysis of Economic Equilibrium*. New Haven, CT: Yale University Press.

19 Only if the excess demand for wealth is abated in certain price configurations is there any possibility that the excess supply of final goods and labor can be overcome.

20 By "institutional features" I mean the geography, infrastructure, and demography of the country; the structure of product and labor markets; the legal framework and customary ways of conducting trade, and all other elements of culture. I do not claim that all institutional features must be identified to pin down a path; but some features will be necessary to do so.

21 Ricardo and Malthus assume the wage is equal across all sectors—agriculture, unproductive labor, and manufacturing.

22 Note that Malthus argues that workers have a love of indolence that exceeds their love of luxuries, which implies that the labor supply curve may be

DOI: 10.1057/9781137562210.0006

backward bending for a wage above the level at which all necessaries can be purchased. See footnote 17, Chapter 2.

23 Note that if the increased number of workers in manufacturing is employed in producing capital goods, there will be no shift in output or labor required in the current period.

24 An outcome, it should be noted, Keynes decried as "a disaster to the progress of economics." Keynes, J. M. (1933) *Essays in Biography*, p. 123.

25 Keynes, J. M. (1936) *The General Theory of Employment, Interest and Money*, reprinted in 1973 by the Macmillan Press Ltd., London, p. 32.

26 Robbins, Lionel (1932, 1935, 2nd ed.). *An Essay on the Nature and Significance of Economic Science*. London: Macmillan, p. 15.

27 Becker, Gary S. (1976) *The Economic Approach to Human Behavior*. Chicago: University of Chicago Press, p. 5.

28 Among all economists, Becker is probably one of the most likely to accept that wealth can be an object of maximization; see Becker, Gary S. and George S. Stigler (March 1977) De Gustibus Non Est Disputandum. *The American Economic Review*, 67(2), pp. 76–90.

29 Rabin, Matthew (2013) Incorporating Limited Rationality into Economics. *Journal of Economic Literature*, 51(2), pp. 528–543, 528.

30 Equilibrium occurs when the plans of all economic agents are mutually compatible, given the environment in which they operate.

31 Sutton, John (2000) *Marshall's Tendencies: What Can Economists Know?* Cambridge, MA: The MIT Press, p. 32.

32 "If only Malthus instead of Ricardo, had been the parent stem from which nineteenth-century economics proceeded, what a much wiser and richer place the world would be today! We have laboriously to rediscover and force through the obscuring envelopes of our misguided education what should never have ceased to be obvious." Keynes, *Essays in Biography*, pp. 120–121.

33 See Hollander, Samuel (1992) *Classical Economics*. Toronto: University of Toronto Press, pp. 253–255 for an argument that Keynes's ideas are not related to Malthus. See Kates, Steven.

34 Keynes, *The General Theory of Employment, Interest and Money*, p. 32.

35 Keynes, *Essays in Biography*, p. 123.

36 Ibid., p. 117.

37 Ricardo, *Works and Correspondence*, vols. I–IX, VIII, p. 260.

38 Baran, Paul A. and Paul M. Sweezy (1966) *Monopoly Capital: An Essay on the American Economic and Social Order*. New York: Monthly Review Press. Space constraints do not permit a review of this contribution to the theory of accumulation and secular stagnation.

DOI: 10.1057/9781137562210.0006

Part II

Accumulation and Secular Stagnation in the Contemporary United States

DOI: 10.1057/9781137562210.0007

3
The Theory of Accumulation and Secular Stagnation

Abstract: *Secular stagnation—a condition of low growth and underemployment of resources—can arise when some agents intend never to spend a portion of their income. If savers intend to spend all their income in the future, there is an incentive to invest to meet that future demand. If savers do not plan to spend all their income in the future, the portion of income not intended to be spent is "Accumulation". If Accumulation is correctly anticipated, it will lower expectations of future demand and deter investment, which will cause the economy to operate below full employment. If Accumulation is not correctly anticipated, investment will go on, but will lead to a crisis of over-production in the future, when the anticipated demand fails to materialize.*[1]

Keywords: Accumulation; debt-deflation; Greenspan's conundrum; secular stagnation

Aronoff, Daniel. *A Theory of Accumulation and Secular Stagnation: A Malthusian Approach to Understanding a Contemporary Malaise*. New York: Palgrave Macmillan, 2016. DOI: 10.1057/9781137562210.0008.

> Consumption is the sole end and purpose of all production
>
> —Adam Smith[2]

> All that is contended for is that no nation can possibly grow rich by an accumulation of capital, arising from a permanent diminution of consumption.
>
> —Thomas Robert Malthus[3]

To provide motivation for the theory linking Accumulation to secular stagnation, I review the unexpected breakdown in the transmission of monetary policy that occurred during the late stages of the US housing boom, when long-term interest rates failed to respond to increases in the Fed funds rate. According to the prevailing paradigm of macroeconomics, of which economist Michael Woodford's textbook *Interest and Prices*, is considered an authoritative source, the breakdown was not expected to occur, in the sense that the Fed was supposed to be able to set the maturity curve of nominal interest rates by manipulation of the overnight Fed funds rate. Prof. Woodford explained that:

> ...determination of the overnight interest rate would also have to imply determination of the equilibrium holding return on longer-lived securities, up to a correction for risk; and so determination of the expected future path of overnight interest rates would essentially determine longer-term interest rates.[4]

It is possible to argue, that the Fed had lost control of interest rates ever since the current account deficit took off in the late 1990s. But prior to the period when the Fed began to increase the Fed funds rate in 2004, there was no inconsistency between monetary policy—which aimed at low interest rates—and long-term market interest rates (which were low). That was no longer the case after the Fed began to raise the overnight rate.

1 Greenspan's "conundrum"—the dog that didn't bark

One of the typical features of business cycles is that interest rates are low at the beginning of the expansion and rise (along with price inflation) throughout the expansion.[5] The increase in rates is driven by competition

DOI: 10.1057/9781137562210.0008

among entrepreneurs and companies for a limited pool of savings, labor and capital goods, and by households for consumer goods. The expansion phase often ends when the central bank reacts to the inflationary pressure caused by the increase in demand by ratcheting up its policy interest rate. The increase in borrowing costs renders some projects unprofitable and some borrowers unfinanceable, which causes credit, and employment, to contract. The slowdown in credit growth marks the end of the boom. This view has a long and distinguished tradition. Knut Wicksell first propounded it in the late 1800s; F. A. Hayek refined and deepened the theory in the 1930s.[6]

The core of the Wicksell/Hayek theory of business cycles is the proposition that declines in real interest rates (relative to the expected return on investment) start booms.[7] Investment projects take time to complete and require funding in advance of realizing revenue (workers need to be paid every two weeks etc…). Cheap credit reduces the cost of financing projects, which increases the present value of future earnings. An increase in present value will cause some previously marginal projects to appear profitable. The perception of profitability induces firms to undertake more projects. In our era of consumer borrowing (which virtually did not exist in the 1930s), lower interest rates also enhance the borrowing capacity of households and reduce the amount of future consumption that must be forgone to repay the debt incurred by increasing current consumption. These forces induce investment and consumption to move inversely with real interest rates.[8]

Later on, when rates rise, as they will eventually do, the theory predicts some of those previously marginal projects, which were commenced due to the initially low rates, become unprofitable once more, and are abandoned.[9] When projects are abandoned—think of acres of empty lots and houses at the end of the US housing boom—workers get laid off and remain unemployed until new projects, requiring additional labor, get launched. In the interim, unemployment swells.[10] The longer the boom goes on, according to this theory, the higher inflation will rise and the deeper will be the recession that follows, since the passage of time increases the volume of projects—all of which take time to complete—that are started and then abandoned in the crash. The waste and unemployment caused by the abandonment of uncompleted projects, along with other inefficiencies induced by inflation, provide compelling reasons for the central bank to put a stop to the boom early on by raising interest rates. A US Fed Chairman

DOI: 10.1057/9781137562210.0008

named William Machesney Martin famously stated that the most vital function of the central bank was to "take away the punch bowl" when the party looked to be getting out of hand, so as to limit the amount of overinvestment and inflation, and thereby reduce the severity of the resultant downturn.

Yet, the US housing boom did not match this "typical" fact pattern in one crucial respect. Although real interest rates were low at the onset of the boom and the landscape was littered with abandoned projects at the end of it (which accords with the Wicksell/Hayek theory) once the boom got underway the key benchmark interest rate (the US government constant maturity ten-year treasury yield) did not rise, as the theory predicts it should have. Instead, the ten-year treasury yield increased only modestly at the end of the boom. In fact, its rise at the end of the expansion that took place during the housing boom was the lowest of any post-World War II boom, even though the Fed raised the Fed funds rate, as it had near the end of all prior expansions.

What happened? It was not the case that the Fed did not try to "take away the punch bowl." It began raising the Fed funds rate in mid-2004, but this time long-term rates did not follow suit. The Fed lifted its policy rate over the next two years from 1% to 5% and yet the ten-year treasury yield barely budged. Fed Chairman Alan Greenspan was perplexed; this had never happened before. He called the Fed's inability to influence the ten-year treasury yield a "conundrum."[11] Credit and leverage continued to grow and the issuance of subprime mortgages peaked in 2006/2007 at the same time as the Fed interest rate hit its peak. Mr. Greenspan correctly dismissed a number of explanations that were proposed at the time. He refuted the idea that low inflation expectations had caused long-term equilibrium nominal interest rates to suddenly decline—which might otherwise explain why treasury yields merely treaded water when the Fed funds rate was increased—by noting that inflation expectations had been low for many years prior to the Fed funds rate increase. He refuted the idea that treasury yields failed to rise because the market had already anticipated the rate rise by pointing out that treasury yields did not rise prior to, and therefore in anticipation of, the Fed funds rate increases. Nor, he argued, was it likely that long-term yields failed to react because investors had suddenly become uncertain about the future path of the Fed funds rate. To the contrary, the Fed had begun to provide markets with forward guidance on rates, which meant uncertainty over the future path of interest rates should have been lower

DOI: 10.1057/9781137562210.0008

than ever before. Economist Axel Leijonhufvud pithily summarized the Fed's impotence:

> If you hike the Bank rate 13 or 14 times—I lost count—and the market pays not the slightest attention but leaves the long rate flat, ***how powerful are you really?*** [12]

The fact that long-term interest rates did not rise appreciably toward the end of the housing boom is a central riddle that has—inexplicably—gone mostly unrecognized. It was the "dog that didn't bark," and any satisfactory explanation of the causes of the housing boom must account for it. Why did this boom, which preceded the most spectacular crash and the deepest contraction since the Great Depression, meet its end—insofar as interest rates are concerned—with not a bang, but with a whimper? (Figure 3.1).

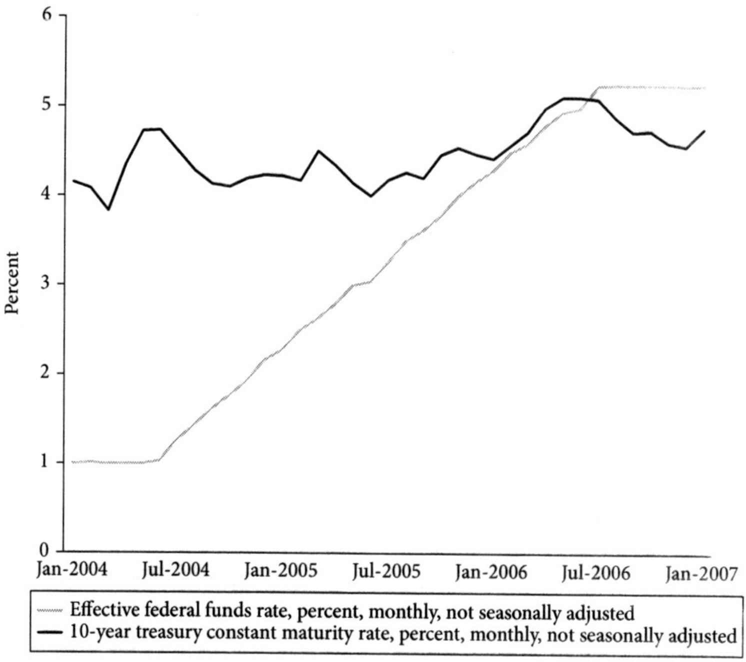

FIGURE 3.1 *The federal funds rate and the ten-year treasury yield (2004–2007)*
Source: Board of Governors of the Federal Reserve System.

DOI: 10.1057/9781137562210.0008

2 Defining "Accumulation" and "secular stagnation"

I will show that the type of current account deficit that emerged in the United States after the turn of the millennium—a product of its large size and its mercantilist origin—introduced a new and historically unprecedented element into the US economy, and that this element may have been magnified by the concurrent re-emergence of a significant concentration of income among a small group of US residents. This new element explains the "jobless" recovery from the 2001 recession, the ongoing stagnation in US employment for years after the onset of the financial crisis and the stagnation in non-housing US investment spending since the turn of the millennium. The essential idea, which comes from Malthus, is that an excess of saving can materialize if people and institutions that accumulate a large share of income have a high propensity to save and do not intend to spend all of their savings in the future. The saving behavior of these groups will cause a deficiency of demand that will either materialize early on, if firms anticipate a shortfall of future demand and curtail their investment plans, or it will occur later on after the investment projects have been completed and the lack of sales cause borrowers to default, triggering a crisis. The theory outlined here is essentially a generalized version of the Malthus theory described in Chapters 1 and 2.

Accumulation and secular stagnation

I define *Accumulation* as an act of saving by someone who does not intend to spend the savings in the future. Such a person or entity is an "accumulator." Secular stagnation has been used in different—though related—ways by different authors. I define *secular stagnation* as a condition in which resources—including labor—are not fully employed, and in which the trend growth rate of the economy is below its potential (i.e. the rate that could be achieved if resources were fully employed). The origin of the linkage between Accumulation and secular stagnation is to be found in Book II of Malthus's *Principles of Political Economy* (1836), where it is stated:

> ...an inordinate passion for accumulation must inevitably lead to a supply of commodities beyond what the structure and habits of such a society will permit to be profitably consumed.[13]

DOI: 10.1057/9781137562210.0008

3 Accumulation and deflation

Consider an economy initially operating at full employment where all agents behave in accordance with the Permanent Income Hypothesis (a concept that is defined in Chapter 4), which means they plan to spend all that they save. Suppose some group suddenly decides it is never going to spend (or give away to charity) a portion of its savings. The members of this group are accumulators, since they desire to accumulate wealth for its own sake, not to spend it. The increase in "permanent" saving—which I have called "Accumulation"—will impact interest rates, employment, and the price level in the following manner.

Assuming the market understands that Accumulation has just shot up, at preexisting interest rates, the increase in Accumulation will reduce the demand for future goods roughly by the amount of the Accumulation, since accumulators have withdrawn that amount from future demand. However, the rise in Accumulation will create an excess supply of saving relative to investment at preexisting interest rates and thereby cause interest rates to decline, which will prompt an increase in borrowing—for investment and consumption. This occurs because the decline in interest rates transfers wealth from savers (among whom are accumulators) to borrowers (who are, by definition, non-accumulators[14]). The transfer of wealth away from accumulators will increase demand, possibly by enough to fully offset the decline from accumulators. But if the increase in Accumulation is large enough, it is possible that interest rates will be pushed to their lower bound and spending might still be below the level consistent with full employment. There must be a lower bound, since interest rates cannot fall below zero, provided agents have the option of holding zero yielding money. Therefore, an accumulation that is large enough to drive interest rates to their lower bound will create a deficiency in demand at preexisting prices. The deficiency in demand will set in motion deflationary forces.

The process of deflation will cause employment to fall for three distinct reasons. One reason is that prices and wages tend to be "sticky"; they do not adjust quickly to reductions in demand. When the decline in spending exceeds the decline in wages and prices, unit sales have to decline.[15] This is so because the decline in spending on goods exceeds the decline in the cost to produce goods. To make this point intuitive, think of a situation where spending falls by 10% and goods prices do

DOI: 10.1057/9781137562210.0008

not change at all. In that case the money spent could purchase no more than 90% of the goods that were formerly purchased. A decline in sales will ultimately lead to a decline in employment, since firms would become bankrupt if they indefinitely produce goods they cannot sell. To approach this issue from the other direction, if wages do not change but prices are flexible and decline in reaction to a reduction in demand, the decline in prices will reduce firms' profit margins. This will create an incentive for firms to lay off workers, and if the reduction in price is large enough, firms will operate at a loss. When that occurs firms are forced to lay off workers in order to avoid bankruptcy. There can be many reasons for sticky wages and prices. Economists have been debating the matter at least since the time of Malthus and Ricardo, nearly two centuries ago. I shall not venture into that debate because for my purpose, what matters is the fact that wages and prices are slow to adjust, not the reasons why.

Nevertheless, prices do eventually decline, even if slowly, when the economy contracts. Many economists contend that unemployment is caused by the inability of wages and prices to adjust rapidly in reaction to a decline in spending. In the example above, if all wages and prices declined by 10%, full employment could be maintained with workers earning the preexisting real wage and firms earning the preexisting real profit.[16] Yet, this line of reasoning does not take account of the interaction of lower prices with long-term debt that is fixed in nominal money terms. When debt is taken into account, it does not follow that the economy will move toward full employment once wages and prices have declined.

This leads to the second reason that deflation causes employment to fall, which a late 19th-/early 20th-century economist named Irving Fisher first articulated. Fisher points out that, since loans are usually required to be repaid in fixed (let us say) dollar amounts, deflation increases the "real" burden of debt, as borrowers earn less money but are required to pay a fixed dollar amount on their indebtedness. The attempt to pay off debts as income is falling requires borrowers to reduce their spending out of income by an ever increasing amount, which intensifies the deflationary pressure. This results in a vicious circle, where deflation begets reduced spending to pay off debts, which begets more deflation. Fisher thinks that this is the primary cause of economic depression. Here is how Fisher describes the process of "Debt

DOI: 10.1057/9781137562210.0008

Deflation" in his celebrated 1933 article titled "*The Debt Deflation Theory of Great Depressions*":

> ... deflation caused by the debt reacts on the debt. Each dollar of debt still unpaid becomes a bigger dollar, and if the overindebtedness with which we started was great enough, the liquidation of debts cannot keep up with the fall of prices, which it causes. In that case, the liquidation defeats itself. While it diminishes the number of dollars owed, it may not do so as fast as it increases the value of each dollar owed. Then, the very effort of individuals to lessen their burden of debts increase it, because of the mass effect of the stampede to liquidate in selling each dollar owed. Then we have the great paradox, which, I submit, is the chief secret of most, if not all, great depressions: the more the debtors pay, the more they owe. The more the economic boat tips, the more it tends to tip. It is not tending to right itself, but is capsizing.[17]

Fisher's insight holds when it is asset prices, rather than goods prices, that deflate. In that case, which occurred during the US financial crisis, the reduction in spending is caused by the effects of deflated asset prices on borrowers and banks. Borrowers are either forced to liquidate unencumbered assets to pay off debts or are denied credit because they lack the collateral (i.e. unencumbered assets of sufficient value) to support new loans. Lenders must write down the value of their loans when collateral values deflate, which depletes their capital and forces them to refrain from new lending. The forced liquidations and contraction in lending cause asset prices to deflate further, which compels borrowers to rein in spending due to the negative wealth effect, the loss of income from liquidated assets and reduced borrowing possibilities. The process is intensified if lenders become fearful and lower the leverage level at which they are willing to lend against collateral, which causes lending of contract further, which creates additional pressure to reduce asset prices, as possibilities for refinancing or obtaining loans to pay off debts become more constricted.

An increase in Accumulation, or in the market's awareness of it, can spark a decline in asset prices. This occurs because the decline in future demand reduces the estimated future revenue from capital goods. The downward pressure on asset prices links Accumulation to Fisher's insight. The link between Accumulation and asset price declines is an additional channel leading from Accumulation to contraction of output, which is operative even if the monetary authorities successfully avert deflation in goods prices.

DOI: 10.1057/9781137562210.0008

For several decades Fisher's idea was dismissed by economists, who reasoned that the repayment of debt merely transferred purchasing power from one group—borrowers—to another group—lenders.[18] Even if, as is often assumed (without foundation), lenders have a lower propensity to spend than do borrowers,[19] a marginal difference in spending propensities is unlikely to account for the cataclysmic decline in spending required to bring about a depression. And besides, the lenders may turn around and re-lend the loan repayments to other high spending borrowers. However, there has been a re-appraisal and extension of Fisher's idea, which economists now consider a core cause of economic contraction.[20] The fundamental insight is that a decline in asset prices implies a decline in wealth for everyone in the economy; borrowers and lenders alike. When a borrower defaults on his loan payment, as he will do when his nominal income and wealth declines to a point where he is unable to generate sufficient funds from her income or from re-leveraging or liquidating his assets to pay off the loan, the lender suffers both a decline in cash flow and a decline in the value of its loan collateral. Both variables will force the lender to contract the issuance of new loans, and highly leveraged intermediaries such as banks may quickly become insolvent. That is how debt–deflation forces lenders to contract credit just as borrowers are contracting their spending.[21]

The third problem created by deflation, when interest rates are at their lower bound, is that deflation increases real interest rates. The real interest rate on a debt is, roughly, the contract interest rate minus the average rate of inflation during the term of the debt. It represents the rate of discount at which lenders are willing to pay, at the inception of the loan, for the purchasing power commanded by the money at the time interest payments and loan repayment is made. To illustrate this point, consider a one-year loan with a 3% yield, payable at maturity. If the price level one year hence is unchanged, the purchasing power at the time of repayment has been discounted at 3%. If the price level one year hence is 3% higher, the purchasing power at the time of repayment has been discounted at 0%, since the purchasing power of the money the lender receives upon repayment is the same as the purchasing power of the money at the inception of the loan. Now suppose the price level one year hence is 3% lower. In that case the real interest rate on the 3% loan is 6%, because the lender is paid 3% more money than he lent, and the purchasing power of the money in which he is repaid has increased by 3%. The increase in real interest rates will shift wealth back toward accumulators—who tend to be lenders—which will cause a decline in investment and consumption. That is why deflation is not a cure for a contraction caused by Accumulation, even where debt-deflation is not present.

Finally, Accumulation creates the problem that, even at a lower price level, after the deflationary process has ended, debts are repaid or restructured, and interest rates are low, spending may still be too low to support full employment. If accumulators are present, there is no evident market adjustment that can restore full employment.[22]

Summary

A significant rise in Accumulation will set in motion forces leading to a decline in nominal interest rates and deflation in goods and asset prices, and the process of deflation will push the economy into contraction. This does not mean that a rise in Accumulation will always lead to deflation, just that it will create a force pushing the economy in that direction. There may be other, countervailing forces, including responses by government, that prevent the deflation from occurring. Moreover, since Accumulation reduces future demand, the near-term impact will be affected by whether or not agents correctly anticipate the future shortfall in demand. This underscores that one must be cautions in drawing conclusions without information about the institutional structure of the economy and the expectations of its participants, which can differ by time and place. Accumulation may also be tempered by price changes, as when declining interest rates (above zero) shift wealth away from accumulators. More generally, there may be price configuration at which Accumulation is eliminated. It all depends on the how the accumulator reacts to changes in his environment.

Nevertheless, for the sets of prices at which Accumulation takes place, there is no equilibrium for the economy to hone in on and the economy may move further away from full employment.

4 How Accumulation accommodates booms

Accumulation involves an increase in saving that is not intended to be spent in the future. If it is properly understood by the market, it

DOI: 10.1057/9781137562210.0008

will cause a reduction in investment and set in motion deflationary forces in asset and goods prices. However, if it is not properly understood that future demand will be reduced Accumulation can ignite an unsustainable boom in the sense that future goods will be produced for which there will be no demand (or insufficient demand to cover the costs of producing them).[23] The boom is fueled by the availability of an enlarged pool of savings looking for places to invest. With incorrect anticipations, firms fail to recognize that a portion of current saving implies reduced demand in the future and they continue to invest in the false belief that today's savers will be tomorrow's consumers; and households borrow in the expectation of earning higher future wages. However, eventually, when firms discover they cannot sell all of the goods they have produced, their shortfall in sales will cause them to curtail investment, and many firms will default on their debt. Likewise, households will be forced to default on debt when anticipated future earnings fail to materialize. Either way, Accumulation leads to deflation and, if leverage is high, to Fisher's "debt-deflation" spiral, whether or not it is correctly anticipated. I shall explain in the next chapter how the rise in Accumulation was quite possibly the ultimate source of boom and bust dynamics that underlay the dotcom boom and the housing boom.

5 Accumulation and Say's principle

The theory of Accumulation can be summarized as the effects on output, employment, and growth caused by a chronic excess demand for wealth assets, which is implied by "an act of saving by someone who does not intend to spend the savings in the future." As was demonstrated in Chapter 2, the non-satiation principle does not hold in such an economy which means it is plagued by a deficiency in demand for final goods and labor that prevents it from operating at full employment on a sustainable basis.[24] The general idea of Accumulation is independent of the institutional structure of an economy. Thus, it can apply to the England of the early 19th century as persuasively as it can apply to the contemporary United States or China. Say's Principle always holds true when considering all tradable items (because it is a truism), but the law of markets, which says that notional excess demands for final goods sums to zero, upon which so much of economic theory rests, does not hold true in the presence of Accumulation.

Identity (3.1) breaks up the inter-temporal budget equation of the accumulator into notional excess demand for final goods and labor (left side) and notional excess demand for wealth (right side), using the notation from Chapter 2. Since an accumulator by definition saves more than he intends to spend, his notional excess demand for wealth is positive, which implies, by Say's Principle, that his notional excess demand for final goods and labor is negative (and of the same absolute value). If all other agents behave in accordance with the non-satiation principle, and have a zero notional excess demand for wealth, it follows that an economy with accumulators has a notional excess supply of goods and labor.

Final Goods and Labor Wealth

$$\sum_{i=0}^{N-3} \sum_{t=0}^{\infty} PntXntk \equiv -\left(\sum_{i=N-2}^{N} \sum_{t=0}^{\infty} PntXntk\right) \qquad (3.1)$$

As with the discussion of the intuitive dynamics of adjustment in Chapter 2, the general point is that, in an economy where everyone obeys the non-satiation principle and wages, prices, and production arrangements are flexible, it is plausible that a full employment equilibrium exists and that the economy hones in on it.[25] When, on the other hand, Accumulation is present, the economy will suffer from a chronic deficiency in demand for goods and labor which cannot be cured by movement of prices (at least within price configurations where Accumulation holds) and there will be no full employment equilibrium. Moreover, no pattern of movement of the economy can be predicted without additional information on its institutional structure and the expectations of its various agents. Intuitively however, one would expect a notional excess supply of good to create pressure for contraction in both the volume of goods transacted and the price. This intuition arises from the simple observation that if, at any given price, the volume of supply offered exceeds the volume of purchase offers for a given good, sellers will be disappointed and, ultimately financially pressed to reduce the supply and the offer price.

The idea of Accumulation does not fit comfortably with modern economic theory. Macroeconomic models require the non-satiation principle in order to determine a stable resting point (or trajectory) of

DOI: 10.1057/9781137562210.0008

the economy—which economists call the "equilibrium" of the economic system. Determining the equilibrium, and its movement in response to changes in the parameters of the model, is the basic concept used by economists to explain and to predict economic phenomena. Accumulation is problematic to economists because it involves a violation of the non-satiation principle because by definition accumulators do not spend all that they earn.

6 Accumulation and Keynesian unemployment

Keynes challenges the notion that markets always gravitate toward full employment equilibrium. As I have posited with Accumulation, Keynes describes an excess of saving over investment as the cause of deflation and unemployment. There are principally two strands to Keynes's thinking about involuntary unemployment, which is a state where a person willing to work at the prevailing wage for his skill level is unable to find employment. Both strands identify the problem as a failure of the market economy to make the adjustments necessary to restore full employment.

One strand of Keynes's thinking about unemployment, which has been notably revived by Nobel Laureate economist Paul Krugman after Japan fell into deflation in the 1990s, has to do with the interaction of depressed animal spirits with the inability of interest rates to drop beneath a lower bound.[26] Keynes's original idea that liquidity preference would suspend riskless interest rates considerably above zero (as discussed in Chapter 2) has been discarded by economists, and it is the zero lower bound that is usually meant by liquidity trap when it is mentioned. A decline in optimism will reduce investment, because investors and entrepreneurs estimate lower potential profits, or are less willing to take on risks. If the economy is operating below full employment when interest rates drop to their lower bound, the deflationary forces described above will kick in. It will do so because excess desired saving implies that spending—on final goods and investment—is below income. In this situation the economy is forced to contract until income declines to a level where it is equal to spending. Income must, by definition, be matched by spending. This is the Keynesian liquidity trap. The concept of Accumulation adds nothing to Keynes's story of how the economy operates in a liquidity trap, but there is a

DOI: 10.1057/9781137562210.0008

crucial difference in the interpretations of what caused the economy to descend into liquidity trap. Both theories attribute the proximate cause to an excess of planned saving over investment, resulting from pessimism over future demand. The difference is that Keynes believes the pessimistic projections usually reflect an error, whereas the theory of Accumulation implies that future demand will decline as Accumulation increases.

The distinction between pessimism caused by depressed animal spirits and low expectations caused by accurate forecasts of declining future demand, affects how an economy in liquidity trap will respond to fiscal stimulus. The essential difference is that a government generated increase in demand[27] might have the effect of restoring optimism, which in the case of liquidity trap arrived at by depressed animal spirits will kick-start the private sector and enable it to operate at full employment without requiring ongoing stimulus. If the liquidity trap is caused by Accumulation, by contrast, stimulus will be less likely to boost optimism and if it does succeed in doing so, it will lead to an unsustainable boom that will be followed by a crisis of overproduction.

The other strand in Keynes's thought about unemployment, which has been articulated by economist Axel Leijonhufvud, has to do with the dynamics of labor market adjustment in the presence of high unemployment.[28] Keynes believes that an economy can get stuck in low employment equilibrium because there is no reliable market mechanism to register what an unemployed person would purchase if he were employed and had income to spend. There is no device to coordinate hiring among all firms, and there are few markets for trading future goods. Involuntary unemployment occurs when firms do not perceive there to be sufficient potential demand—generated from the wages paid to new hires and the profits earned from their contribution to output—to justify hiring more workers. If the workers were employed, they would spend their income on current and future goods, but no worker would spend all her income at the firm that hired her. Therefore, even if firms understood the spending habits of workers, no individual firm would have an incentive to hire an additional worker, unless it was otherwise optimistic about the potential for growing its sales.[29]

The paucity of futures markets means that most firms cannot book sales in advance and therefore must guess at future demand when setting current production plans. This requires firms to guess at the effects current

DOI: 10.1057/9781137562210.0008

saving will have on future demand, and the effects that increased employment will have on current and future demand. Keynes makes this point in connection with interpreting the impact of current saving on demand:

> An act of individual saving means—so to speak—a decision not to have dinner today. But it does not necessitate a decision to have dinner or to buy a pair of boots a week hence or a year hence or to consume any specified thing at any specified date. Thus it depresses the business of preparing today's dinner without stimulating the business of making ready for some future act of consumption... If saving consisted not merely in abstaining from present consumption but in placing simultaneously a specific order for future consumption, the effect might indeed be different. For in that case the expectation of some future yield from investment would be improved, and the resources released from preparing for present consumption would be turned over to preparing for the future consumption...[30]

The inability to contract for future delivery of goods is an impediment to achieving full employment in a market economy when animal spirits are depressed. It underscores the economy's reliance upon sui generis beliefs about the future.[31] But Keynes does not doubt the existence of full employment equilibrium. That is the source of his optimism that a government fiscal stimulus can kick-start a movement toward full employment. Where Accumulation is present, the prognosis is more pessimistic. Missing markets and/or the liquidity trap may keep the economy away from full employment, but government stimulus will not be sufficient to guide it toward full employment if private spending cannot ultimately be raised. In that case, as has been seen, there will not be a full employment equilibrium to hone in on.

7 Accumulation and productivity growth

Productivity is measured as the value of final product produced by some measurable units of labor and capital goods used in the production process. Accumulation reduces the demand for—and therefore the price of—final output. Therefore, Accumulation will reduce the productivity of labor and other capital goods used in production at any given level of output.[32] This means that the decline in productivity growth that gathered pace after the turn of the millennium, which coincided with the growth of Accumulation, may have been (at least partly) caused by Accumulation.

DOI: 10.1057/9781137562210.0008

8 Conclusion

This chapter opened with a review of Greenspan's "conundrum," which provided motivation to propose a theory explaining how Accumulation sets in motion deflationary forces. It was shown that Accumulation operates in the way Malthus envisioned, and that the concept can be placed in a more general setting. In particular, it was argued that an economy plagued by Accumulation does not have a full employment equilibrium and therefore cannot be described using the tools of equilibrium analysis. The extent to which Accumulation affects an economy is determined by the same factors that were debated by Malthus and Ricardo; the degree of price flexibility and the extent to which some agents save without any intention of ever spending. A new element, not considered by either Malthus or Ricardo was introduced; the interaction of deflation caused by Accumulation with legacy debt, which pushes the economy further away from full employment.

Chapter 4 will explore the forces of Accumulation that entered the US economy in the 2000s and the role those novel forces had in increasing volatility and moving the US economy toward secular stagnation. It will be seen that Accumulation was the ultimate cause of the housing boom and that the concept can be applied to resolve Greenspan's "conundrum."

Notes

1 After completion of the final draft of this chapter, the author became aware of an earlier paper that anticipated the essential ideas of this chapter. The author wishes to acknowledge Palley, Thomas (March 1993) Under-Consumption and the Accumulation Motive. *Journal of Radical Political Economics*, 25, pp. 71–86.

2 Malthus, Thomas Robert (1836) *Principles of Political Economy, second edition*, reprinted by August M. Kelly, New York (1964), pp. 322 and 326.

3 Smith, Adam (1776) *The Wealth of Nations*, Modern Library Edition. New York, NY: Random House Inc., 1994. Modern Library Edition, p. 715.

4 Woodford, Michael (2003) *Interest and Prices: Foundations of a Theory of Monetary Policy*. Princeton, NJ: Princeton University Press, p. 37.

5 The preceding sentence should be interpreted as referring to nominal rates of interest and inflation relative to trend. Therefore, a given rate of interest or inflation could be low, if trend rates of interest or inflation were high; or high, if trend rates of interest or inflation were low.

DOI: 10.1057/9781137562210.0008

6 See Wicksell, Knut (1936) *Interest and Prices*. London: Macmillan Ltd.; Hayek, F. A. (1933) *Monetary Theory and the Trade Cycle*. London: Jonathan Cape Ltd.; Hayek, F. A. (1967) *Prices and Production*. New York: August M. Kelly.

7 If animal spirits are elevated at the start of a boom—and it is almost inconceivable that a boom could commence in the absence of elevated animal spirits—then it might require no more than a small decline in interest rates to spark an expansion. Another variable not discussed in the text is that risk spreads will typically compress at the beginning of a boom—another dimension of elevated optimism—which represents a reduction in borrowing costs.

8 The effect of interest rates on consumption is a core driver of economic fluctuations of the contemporary "New Keynesian" models of the economy, which posits that sluggish adjustments of wages and prices to exogenous shocks to the underlying conditions of supply and demand in sectors of the economy can be offset by central bank adjustment of nominal interest rates. For example, a shock that causes income to contract can be offset by a reduction in nominal interest rates, since (1) sluggish wage/price adjustment ensures the nominal reduction will be a real reduction (at least for some time), and (2) the reduction in real interest rates will induce consumers to increase current spending, by reducing the amount of future consumption that must be foregone to indulge in an increase in current consumption. Thus, the impact of interest rates on economic activity in New Keynesian models is quite similar to their effects in the Wicksell/Hayek model. See Clarida, Richard, Jordi Gali, and Mark Gertler (December 1999) The Science of Monetary Policy: A New Keynesian Perspective. *Journal of Economic Literature*, XXXVII, pp. 1661–1707.

9 This is an oversimplification of Hayek's theory. He argues that lower interest rates increase the profitability of more time-consuming production processes, and therefore induces a lengthening of many production processes. The profitability of longer-term projects is more sensitive to changes in interest rates. Therefore, the lengthening of production processes undertaken during the boom magnifies the negative impact on profits of the eventual rise in interest rates, which increases the volume of projects that must be abandoned at the end of the boom, and thereby deepens the recession that follows.

10 The dynamics of the Wicksell/Hayek theory fits the data on labor market behavior. When the economy goes into recession, layoffs rise relative to job vacancies. When it recovers, vacancies rise relative to layoffs.

11 Mr. Greenspan made that remark in his February 17, 2005, testimony before the US Senate Committee on Banking, Housing, and Urban Affairs.

12 Leijonhufvud, Axel (2007) *So far from Ricardo, So close to Wicksell*. Paper given at the 2007 Jornadas Monetarias y Bancarias, Central Bank of Argentina,

DOI: 10.1057/9781137562210.0008

June 4–5, session on "Trade-off between Monetary and Financial Stability." p. 6. http://www-ceel.economia.unitn.it/staff/leijonhufvud/files/axel4.pdf

13 Malthus, Thomas Robert (1836) *Principles of Political Economy*, second edition, reprinted by Augustus M. Kelley, New York, 1964, p. 325.

14 A more general statement would allow for the possibility that, among borrowers, are people who are accumulators. This might occur with young persons borrowing to pay for schooling and so on, who will nevertheless earn more in their lifetime than they plan to spend.

15 Assuming a constant markup of goods prices over-production costs.

16 Real wages and profits refer to the purchasing power of the nominal money—wage and profit. If all prices declined by 10%, then a worker earning 10% less wages could purchase exactly the same bundle of goods as she could before the reduction in spending.

17 Fisher, Irving (October 1933) The Debt Deflation Theory of Great Depressions. *Econometrica*, 1(4), pp. 337–357.

18 [Fisher's] diagnosis led him to urge President Roosevelt to subordinate exchange-rate considerations for the need for reflation, advice that (ultimately) FDR followed. Fisher's idea was less influential in academic circles, though, because of the counterargument that debt-deflation represented no more than a redistribution from one group (debtors) to another (creditors). Absent implausibly large differences in marginal spending propensities among the groups, it was suggested, pure redistributions should have no significant macroeconomic effects. Bernanke, Ben S. (February 1995) The Macroeconomics of the Great Depression: A Comparative Approach. *Journal of Money, Credit, and Banking*, 27(1), p. 17.

19 There are no grounds to assert, prima facie, in a fractional reserve banking system, that borrowers have higher propensities than depositors. It may be the other way round! The liquidity transformation performed by banks enables high spenders to temporarily deposit unspent funds. The deposits, as is well understood, are then re-lent to borrowers for longer duration.

20 Ben Bernanke led the re-appraisal of Fisher's idea and emphasized the balance sheet channel of propagating distress into the economy. See Bernanke, Ben S. (June 1983) Nonmonetary Effects of the Financial Crisis in Propagation of the Great Depression. *American Economic Review*, 73, pp. 257–276. Richard Koo has become the leading contemporary advocate of the debt-deflation theory, which he has re-labeled "balance sheet recession." See Koo, Richard (2014) Escape from *Balance Sheet Recession and the QE Trap: A Hazardous Road for the World Economy*. Hoboken, NJ: John Wiley.

21 Several additional costs flow from the contraction in lending, including the costs of reorganizing bankrupt borrowers and banks, and the decline in new ventures or the expansion of existing ones. As an example, Ricardo Caballero and his colleagues showed how, in Japan in the 1990s, banks continued

DOI: 10.1057/9781137562210.0008

lending to zombie borrowers, with dim prospects for profitable investment, in order to avoid the realization of the loan losses on their accounting books. Channeling loans to zombie borrowers diverted the flow of savings away from productive investments and deterred entry into the industries occupied by the subsidized zombies. Both effects reduced economic growth and job creation. See Caballero, Ricardo J., Takeo Hoshi, and Anil K. Kashyap (2008) Zombie Lending and Depressed Restructuring in Japan. *American Economic Review*, 98(5), pp. 1943–1977.

22 It is tempting to conjecture that the decline in wealth engendered by Accumulation will cure it. That is what Keynes believes will occur, which is what he has in mind in his description of the "Euthanasia of the Rentier." But it is also possible that a decline in wealth will motivate accumulators to reduce spending further, in order to maintain their targeted bequests. It all depends on motives, about which economic theory has nothing at all to say; and upon which empirical studies have not—to this author's knowledge—shed light.

23 Note that an increase in Accumulation does not have to be accompanied by an increase in aggregate saving. For example, Accumulation can be increased by an increase in accumulators' share of existing savings. Furthermore, since a shift in a fixed pool of saving toward accumulators implies an absolute decline in the demand for future goods, a continuation of the preexisting level of investment will constitute an unsustainable boom.

24 All that is required to establish that all income is spent on final goods is to assume that agents will always desire at least one more increment of some good (in preference to wealth accumulation). If that is so, people will always want to spend whatever extra money they have to acquire more of that good. In order to ensure that equilibrium exists, economic models include this assumption. Note that Accumulation might take place for certain sets of price vectors and not others. For example, if the prices of all assets of accumulators fell to near zero, they might no longer behave as accumulators. There is, however, no prima facie guarantee that a full employment equilibrium exists at such prices.

25 It must be said, however, that economists have not been successful in modeling behavior when the economy is out of equilibrium—even where an equilibrium set of prices exist. For a well-respected, but unsuccessful, attempt to grapple with the problem, see Fisher, Franklin (1983) *Disequilibrium Foundations of Equilibrium Economics*. Cambridge, UK: Cambridge University Press.

26 See Krugman, Paul (1998) *It's Baaack: Japan's Slump and the Return of the Liquidity Trap*. Brookings Papers on Economic Activity, Vol. 2. Washington, DC: Brookings Institution, pp. 137–204.

DOI: 10.1057/9781137562210.0008

27 The concept of stimulating demand includes Krugman's suggestion of credibly setting a future inflation target. See Krugman, *It's Baaack*, pp. 137–204.

28 See Leijonhufvud, Axel (1981) The Wicksell Connection: Variations on a Theme. In *Information and Coordination: Essays on Macroeconomic Theory*. New York: Oxford University Press, pp. 131–203.

29 Notably, Malthus makes precisely this point: No fresh hands can be employed in any sort of industry merely in consequence of the demand for its produce occasioned by the persons employed... There must be something in the previous state of the demand and supply of the commodity in question, or in its price, antecedent to and independent of the demand occasioned by the new laborers, in order to warrant the employment of an additional number of people in its production. Malthus, *Principles of Political Economy*, reprinted *second edition*, p. 312.

30 Keynes, J. M. (1936) *The General Theory of Employment, Interest and Money*, pp. 210–211, London: Macmillan Press, Ltd, 1973.

31 Of course, the problem is not solved by futures markets if people do not know what they will want in the future. In that case—which seems realistic—people would choose not to contract for most items even if given the opportunity to do so. The deep reason why there are so few futures markets is that there are few people who would use them.

32 This does not imply that Accumulation will reduce actual productivity. If Accumulation reduces employment, the smaller workforce may be more productive, which will increase actual productivity.

DOI: 10.1057/9781137562210.0008

4

Accumulation and Secular Stagnation in the United States after the Turn of the Millennium

Abstract: *A US current account deficit implies that foreigners spend less in the US than they earn from the US. If they intend not to increase their US spending in the future, they are accumulators. The mercantilist policies of Southeast Asia and China, which involved hoarding dollar assets to build up buffer reserves and to support undervalued currencies, was a form of accumulation. They did not intend to spend their dollar savings, for doing so would undermine their objectives. Top income earners who intend to leave large bequests to their heirs are also Accumulators. Mercantilist driven current account deficits and income concentration both increased markedly in the 2000's. The resultant Accumulation lowered US trend growth and increased volatility; a predicament that has been called "secular stagnation".*

Keywords: Chinese saving; current account deficit; income concentration; permanent income hypothesis; Mercantilism; safe asset shortage

Aronoff, Daniel. *A Theory of Accumulation and Secular Stagnation: A Malthusian Approach to Understanding a Contemporary Malaise.* New York: Palgrave Macmillan, 2016. DOI: 10.1057/9781137562210.0009.

DOI: 10.1057/9781137562210.0009

> If you go back and you study the economy prior to the crisis, there's something a little bit odd. Many people believe that monetary policy was too easy. Everybody agrees that there was a vast amount of imprudent lending going on. Almost everybody believes that wealth, as it was experienced by households, was in excess of its reality. Too easy money, too much borrowing, too much wealth. Was there a great boom? Capacity utilization wasn't under any great pressure. Unemployment wasn't under any remarkably low level. Inflation was entirely quiescent. So somehow, even a great bubble wasn't enough to produce any excess in aggregate demand.
>
> —Lawrence Summers[1]

> Practically it has always been found that the excessive wealth of the few is in no respect equivalent with regard to effectual demand, to the more moderate wealth of the many.
>
> —Thomas Robert Malthus[2]

In the last chapter I articulated a theory that relates Accumulation to secular stagnation and output volatility. In this chapter, I explain that foreign mercantilists and people who spend below their income during their lifetime are accumulators. In so doing, I argue that Accumulation is the ultimate force behind the pattern of volatility and below trend growth in output and employment that the US economy had been subjected to since the late 1990s. Finally, I resolve the mystery of the "dog that didn't bark."

1 The current account deficit

The current account deficit and permanent saving

Beginning in the late 1990s, governments of Asian countries undertook large-scale interventions into the currency market to achieve goals that required they accumulate dollar assets. After the Asian financial crisis, Southeast Asian countries accumulated dollar reserves as a buffer stock to cushion (and to deter) any future run on their currencies. Then, starting in the early 2000s China began to accumulate large volumes of dollar assets as a part of a mercantilist policy to promote exports. In

DOI: 10.1057/9781137562210.0009

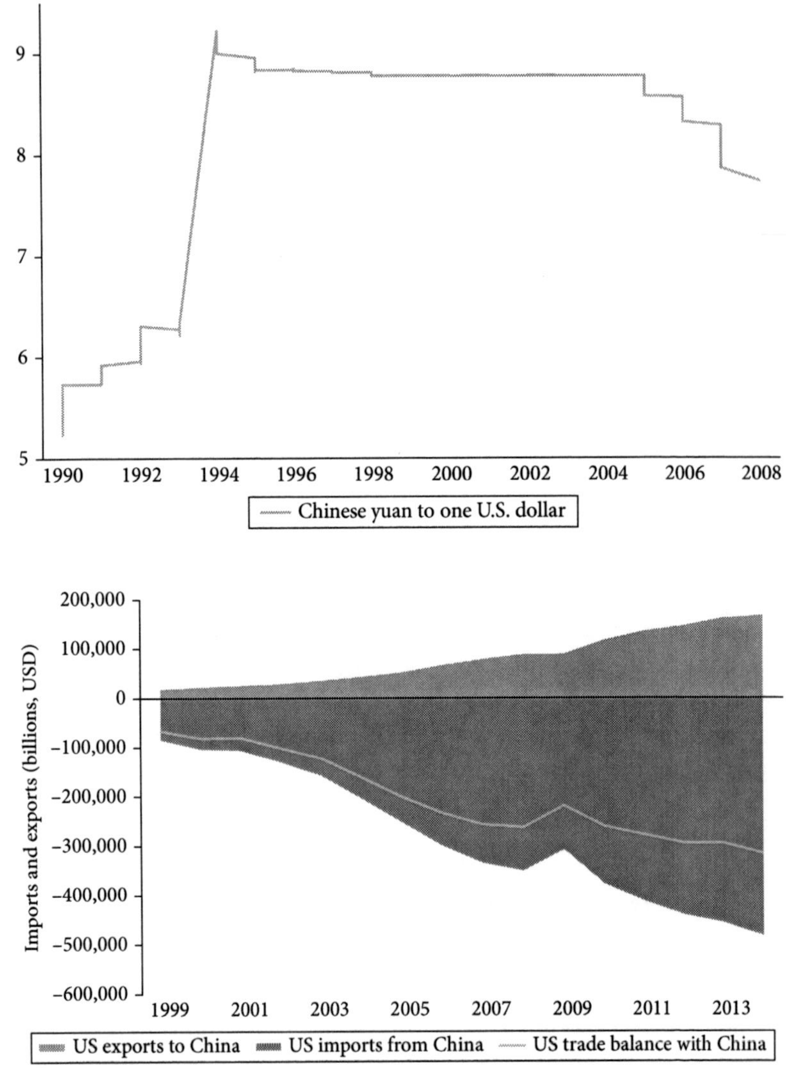

FIGURE 4.1 *The China/US FX rate (1990–2008) and bi-lateral trade balance (1999–2014)*

both cases, the policies pursued by the governments required they not spend their foreign reserves, since spending would undo the effects of the intervention. The buffer stocks accumulated in response to the Asian financial crisis were intended only for spending in the event of a run on the domestic currency.[3] China's mercantilist Accumulation had to be retained, and not spent on US goods, for so long as it wished to promote its net exports.[4,5]

The foreign Accumulation of dollar assets was extremely large. In the 15 years since the onset of the Asian financial crisis, offshore dollar reserves increased by over $1trillion, while the US current account deficit (CAD) soared from 1.5% of GDP to a peak of nearly 7% of GDP in the 3rd quarter of 2006. The common factor between the reaction to the Asian financial crisis and China's mercantilist policy is that, beginning in the late 1990s (as the US trade deficit with Asia took off) its Asian trading partners earned an increasing amount of income from the United States, which they held as savings they never intended to spend. They were engaged in permanent saving.

The US current account deficit as a source of Accumulation

Adam Smith points out that saving is not itself wealth, it is rather an option to acquire the valuable things that comprise wealth. If that option is never exercised, the saver may admire her swelling bank statement, but others will enjoy the goods that the purchasing power of the statement commands. Smith recognizes this when he wrote that "wealth does not consist in money, or in gold and silver; but in what money purchases, and is valuable only for purchasing."[6] It formed his core argument against the policy of mercantilism, which was then, and still is today, practiced by many countries.

Understanding an important concept: mercantilism

A fundamental contention of this chapter is that the origins of the US housing boom and the financial crisis that followed arose, in large part, from the mercantilist policies of China and other Southeast Asian countries. Consequently, it is vital that the reader understand what I mean by the phrase "mercantilism."

In *The Wealth of Nations*, Adam Smith describes the policy of using government intervention to run trade surpluses, as *Mercantilism*.

DOI: 10.1057/9781137562210.0009

> ...the encouragements of exportation, and the discouragement of importation, are the two great engines by which the mercantile system proposes to enrich every country...Its ultimate object [is]...to enrich the country by an advantageous balance of trade.[7]

Therefore, any policy that has as its primary goal to run a current account surplus is "mercantilist." It is explained in what follows that the trade policies of Southeast Asian countries in response to the Asian Financial crisis of 1997, and of China during the 2000s, were mercantilist.

A mercantilist country endeavors to expand its net exports of goods in order to expand output and accumulate foreign reserves (or gold in Smith's day). There are a number of reasons a country might adopt mercantilist polices, which in recent decades have included motivations to deter, or cushion, sudden stops in offshore capital inflows and the desire to expand employment by promoting exports. Smith writes about the desire to accumulate gold, which he derided as an illusory and counter-productive quest to increase wealth. He describes the common belief among the mercantilist countries of his time that "A rich country...is supposed to be a country abounding in money; and to heap up gold and silver in any country is supposed to be the readiest way to enrich it."[8] Smith argued, to the contrary, that mercantilists do not increase their wealth and their workers labor in vain, if they never plan to spend their export earnings on foreign produced goods:

> To attempt to increase the wealth of any country, either by introducing or by detaining in it an unnecessary quantity of gold and silver, is as absurd as it would be to attempt to increase the good cheer of private families, by obliging them to keep an unnecessary number of kitchen utensils.[9]

He observes that the mercantilist country enables other countries to spend beyond their means, while it frugally spends below its means. It does so by subsidizing its producers at the expense of its consumers:

> Consumption is the sole end and purpose of all production...But in the mercantilist system, the interest of the consumer is almost constantly sacrificed to that of the producer; and it seems to consider production, and not consumption, as the ultimate end and object of all industry and commerce.[10]

DOI: 10.1057/9781137562210.0009

In this sense, the mercantilist appears to be the unwitting benefactor of the non-mercantilist. Smith argued that those who accused foreign mercantilists of destroying home economy jobs by selling more goods into the home economy than the home economy exports to the mercantilist country, focused on a superficial attribute. The essential underlying matter, according to Smith, is that the mercantilist sends goods to the home economy while receiving nothing in return, except for options to buy goods that it does not intend to exercise. Smith is not concerned that the shift in spending in favor of imports from the mercantilists might cause a reduction in home economy employment. He is confident that market forces will bring about adjustments in prices, and possibly bring forth monetary substitutes, sufficient to ensure that all resources of the home economy, including labor, will be fully utilized, no matter what its trade balance is. Smith's position issues from his belief that in a market economy, idle resources create profit opportunities for those who can figure out how to employ them to meet unmet desires, and that there is never a shortage of persons eager to make a profit.[11] It is a very compelling argument.

Adam Smith's description of a mercantilist fits my definition of an accumulator—one who does not plan ever to spend all that he has saved. He correctly observed that the accumulator achieves no gain—other than psychic satisfaction—from his abstinence. Yet Smith is, perhaps, too sanguine in his confidence that the non-mercantilist country could readily achieve full employment. Certainly, if the trade imbalance self-corrects, trade cannot be a source of reduced employment in the long run. A market not subject to intervention contains a mechanism by which the terms of trade automatically adjust to re-establish balance when large trade deficits and surpluses develop between countries. When exchange rates float, the deficit country currency will depreciate, which will reduce the foreign currency price of its exports and increase the domestic currency price of its imports. This will shift purchases toward the deficit country and thereby shrink the deficit.[12] When the exchange rate is fixed, the surplus country will experience an inflow of foreign reserves[13] and the surplus country may, if it elects to lend or invest its reserves in deficit country assets—which is called a "capital flow bonanza"—experience an outflow of reserves. These reserve flows will cause the price level in the surplus country to increase relative to the deficit country. This will alter the terms of trade as before, and shrink the imbalance.[14]

DOI: 10.1057/9781137562210.0009

The objective of the mercantilist, as Smith describes it, is to build up foreign reserves. In more recent times, the objective of the mercantilist has been to expand output by maintaining positive net exports. As can be seen in identity (4.1) the one goal implies the other. To achieve either goal, the mercantilist must short-circuit the market adjustment process in order to prevent its current account surplus from shrinking. Figure 4.1 displays the result of the currency intervention employed by China to block the market adjustment process in order to promote its trade surplus with the United States. China fixed the Remnimbi-dollar exchange at an artificially low rate, sterilized the dollar inflows to prevent domestic inflation, and subsidized exporters.[15] The only other avenue for adjustment would have been US deflation, which was successfully avoided.[16] Adam Smith does not adequately explain how, in an economy running a large current account deficit, where the market adjustment process is blocked, market forces are able to replace the hole in demand caused by the current account deficit.

The essence of the matter lies in the Accumulation of the mercantilist. The very act of withdrawing the surplus it earns from future consumption demand, reduces the return on investment. The mercantilist may add to the pool of saving available for home economy investment, if it recycles its surplus back into the home economy through a capital inflow, but its act of permanent saving shrinks the size of the market into which any of the products of investment can later on be sold. In accordance with Say's Principle, the mercantilist's has an excess of wealth accumulation from home economy assets and a deficiency in demand for home economy labor and final goods. This can be expressed by the identity that defines the relationship, during an interval of time, between a home economy current account deficit (CAD) and the corresponding build-up in financial claims from foreign economies. Noting that the CAD is the sum {Trade balance + Net financial transfers + net return on cross border assets}, the relationship is:

$$\text{CAD} \equiv \text{Change in Foreign Net Financial Claims on Home Economy} \qquad (4.1)$$

A foreign mercantilist runs a current account surplus (which is the mirror image of the CAD run by the home economy and reflects a net deficiency in demand for home economy goods and labor) and builds up financial claims in the process. Just as in Table 2.1, those claims can

DOI: 10.1057/9781137562210.0009

be held in the form of money—the currency or central bank reserves of the home economy—or as loans to, or investments in, home economy entities.

A mercantilist does not obey the non-satiation principle. This is the fundamental reason why mercantilism is a negative sum game for market economies. It creates a reduction in consumption and employment in non-mercantilist countries that is not matched by any increase in employment or consumption in the mercantilist country. One might think that the increase in net export boosts employment in the mercantilist country. But in a market economy (assuming non-satiation obtains), the mercantilist would not require a trade surplus to attain full employment. For this reason, economists from Adam Smith's day to the present time have thought it possible to convince the mercantilist that its policy was self-destructive, in the sense that its abstinence from consumption does not generate any increase in employment.

China's mercantilist policies

Smith's argument may not have been persuasive to China in the 2000s, however, which was not a fully market economy. It was a mixed economy plagued by oversaving in the sectors controlled by the state. China required a large current account surplus in order to attain full employment in the 2000s. China had a problem of excess saving, which appears to have been generated by non-market forces stemming from changes in economic policy that were adopted after the Tiananmen Square protests in 1989.

Chinese economic policy underwent a significant change after Tiananmen, as the Communist Party under the leadership of Deng Xiaoping pulled back on many of the freedoms previously granted to domestic enterprise. The government clamped down on the free market reforms in rural areas, bolstered the role of monopoly State-Owned Enterprises (SOEs) in the domestic economy, and re-asserted government control over banking. At the same time, however, China increased its commitment to trade, which Deng endorsed with his famous "Southern Tour" of port cities in 1992. Economist Yasheng Huang described the change in Chinese economic policy this way:

> The prevailing economic policy in the 1990s was to favor the urban areas over the rural areas and to favor foreign capitalists—FDI—over indigenous capitalists. The cumulative effect of all these policies was a dramatic change

DOI: 10.1057/9781137562210.0009

> in the balance of power between the two China's—the rural China that is more capitalistic and market—driven and the urban China that is more state-controlled. In the 1990s the balance tilted decisively in favor of the urban China.[17]

China became a mixed economy. The state dominated certain industries. Factor markets for agriculture and industrial goods—steel, power generation, transportation infrastructure, and land—and banking remained heavily regulated by the state and/or monopolized by SOEs. The state limited investment options for individual savers to residential real estate and bank deposits. Money raised from real estate became a primary source for funding local governments, which were able to confiscate land from peasants and lease to property developers. Deposit interest rates were set at very low levels, and banks were directed to lend to SOEs at low interest rates and to invest in government bonds. The SOEs did not distribute dividends to the state, but rather reinvested earnings in new projects (why they did not distribute dividends is a matter of ongoing speculation). The result of state domination was to divert savings and SOE profits into investment in infrastructure and to promote real estate development. It also reduced factor prices for the rest of the economy, which acted as a subsidy to producers.

Consumer goods markets and export industries operated with far less state regulation and SOE involvement. Low factor prices and low labor costs encouraged production, but the lack of credit—which was channeled to SOEs—required non-state firms to finance investment with retained earnings. The combination of profitable export growth opportunities and limited credit resulted in an extremely high savings rate among private corporations. The limitation on shareholder distributions damped consumer demand, which encouraged the flow of investment toward export industries.

Social insurance spending—for education and healthcare—was reduced, which caused households to increase precautionary savings. The State cut it expenditure on social benefits and SOEs, who offered some level of benefits, rationalized operations, and shed workers. Non-state firms possessed a significant bargaining advantage over the massive wave of rural labor moving to the port cities in search of employment and did not find it necessary to offer fringe benefits to attract employees. The poor bargaining position of rural workers was partially caused by the post-Tiananmen discouragement of rural entrepreneurship, which suppressed rural incomes.

DOI: 10.1057/9781137562210.0009

The post-Tiananmen economic policy reshaped the balance between sectors of the Chinese economy. Exports, infrastructure, and real estate development became the engines of China's economic growth, which were financed by dramatic increases in both corporate and household savings and Foreign direct investment (FDI). Consumer goods industries lagged due to the extremely high rate of saving.[18]

During the 1990s savings, as a proportion of GDP, grew in all sectors: household, business, and government. In 2000 China's savings rate of 37% of GDP was the highest ever recorded for a country. Notwithstanding China's breakneck GDP growth rate, which averaged above 10% from 2000 to 2007,[19] the domestic economy could not profitably invest all of its growing pool of savings. The rate of return on domestic investment in China became very low. China's economy continued to grow, but its growth had become unbalanced between sectors; heavy in basic industries, construction, and real estate, and light in consumer goods and social infrastructure.

The conjuncture of a low return on domestic investment (resultant from the low rate of consumption relative to GDP) and excessive saving created a policy dilemma by the late 1990s. If the savings were not invested, the economy would contract, but if domestic investment continued to grow at its prior trend, there was a risk of massive defaults and bankruptcies. Market opportunities directed investment toward the export sector, where savings could be profitability employed. The increase in the share of investment directed to exports was the fundamental force that propelled China into current account surplus.

In the 2000s, China managed to avoid the contractionary effects of oversaving at least in part by exporting a sizeable proportion of its output and its excess saving abroad. China's external trade had grown steadily since the early 1980s, but in the 2000s trade, and exports in particular, morphed into gargantuan proportions. In 2000 China's export/GDP ratio was around 23%, which was actually below the world average export/GDP ratio of around 25%. By 2007 Chinas export/GDP ratio had grown to over 38.4%, compared to a world average of just under 29%.[20] By the end of the 2000s China had become the largest exporter in the world.

Therefore, China benefitted from its current account surplus insofar as net exports provided a replacement for deficient domestic demand and the capital flow bonanza provided an outlet for its excess saving. In effect, China suffered from the same problem of Accumulation that was identified

DOI: 10.1057/9781137562210.0009

by Malthus. By running a current account surplus (CAD) it managed to export the excess saving offshore, and to generate a matching increase in demand for Chinese goods. The former eliminated the excess demand for wealth, while the latter eliminated the excess supply of goods.

More recently, the bi-lateral trade imbalance has narrowed, so that Chinese mercantilism is not as pressing an issue for the United States now, as it was during the housing boom. But China has not cured its problem of excess saving. If it is no longer able to boost domestic demand with net exports, China will face the contractionary forces that Malthus described. China has experienced remarkable growth since the reform and opening policy was implemented in the late 1970s, and the lifting of nearly one billion persons out of extreme poverty is one of the great events of history. But if China is unable to implement reforms that eliminate its chronic excess saving its growth will languish, for the reasons explained by Malthus.

2 Income concentration

Income concentration and permanent saving

When a person spends less than the income he has earned, the unspent amount is his savings. That is a familiar concept. He must hold his savings in some asset, and except for stuffing mattresses full of dollar bills, it will usually be lent out, invested in securities, or used to purchase durable assets (such as housing, autos, and furniture). That is familiar, too. What may be a somewhat less familiar concept, except to economists, is that people and businesses usually plan to spend most of what they have saved—just later on. The hypothesis is that we want to maximize what we can spend over our lifetime, and to consume as smoothly as possible over time. To achieve this, we borrow (spend more than we earn) when we are young or when we suffer an unexpected temporary decline in income, as from a spell of unemployment, and repay the debts and accumulate savings during our peak earning years, and then spend the remainder in our retirement. It turns out that many of us actually do behave this way, more or less. Nobel Laureate economist Milton Friedman first documented this behavior and ascertained the motive that produced it in the 1950s; he calls the proposition that people aim to spend all of the income earned over their lifetime as evenly as possible the Permanent

DOI: 10.1057/9781137562210.0009

Income Hypothesis (PIH).[21] Another Nobel Laureate economist, Franco Modigliani, found more evidence and refined the theory;[22] many others have followed in their footsteps and further developed the insight in many ways. Friedman's initial hypothesis has endured the test of time—at least until very recently—and the empirical evidence supporting it makes the PIH one of the most robust theories in economics.

One of the implications of Friedman's theory is that the act of saving normally creates future demand. If we are destined to spend all that we have earned during our lifetime, it follows that we *must* in the future spend what we have saved today (plus the interest our savings have earned in the interim). Today's saver is tomorrow's consumer.[23] In an efficient economy, it will be recognized that today's savers will be tomorrow's customers, which will create an incentive for firms to invest the savings to produce goods for future consumption. Therefore, in an efficient economy every dollar saved will be invested to produce future goods. An increase in saving will not cause employment to decline, because the labor no longer needed to produce current consumption goods will instead be needed to produce an increased amount of future goods.[24] Friedman's finding implies that an increase in the rate of saving out of income cannot, by itself, be a cause for economic contraction. If people behave in accordance with the PIH, there cannot be a recession due to underconsumption; the concept of underconsumption or over-saving is meaningless in such a world.[25] So long as agents do not slip their dollars inside their mattresses, and provided the market operates efficiently enough to act on the fact that saving implies future demand, an increase in savings should not affect the level of economic activity; it will just shift the mix of activity away from consumption and toward investment.[26]

One might at this point object that the PIH applies only to individuals (or households) and not to firms or government. This is true, but it does not necessarily alter the conclusion that savings will eventually be spent. Firms ultimately distribute their profits to shareholders, and governments, well the government usually spends everything it collects!

Yet there are important caveats to the theory. Some people do not save. People who live from paycheck to paycheck during their peak earning years are not able to smooth their lifetime spending. Conversely, wealthy people save a great deal and may refrain from spending all that they earn (or inherit) in order to bequeath an estate to their children when they die.[27] In the post World War II era America became a middle-class

DOI: 10.1057/9781137562210.0009

society; the distribution of income became concentrated in the middle. What Friedman documents is the behavior of middle-class people who are wealthy enough to smooth their consumption over time, but not so wealthy as to leave large inheritances to their descendants. When the majority of US citizens were middle class (meaning the middle 50% of income distribution received the majority of income) these exceptions to the PIH were not significant enough to cause the aggregate outcome to deviate from what Friedman predicted. However, times have changed.[28]

Research by Thomas Piketty and Emanuel Saiz indicates that the distribution of income in America has become decidedly less equal in recent decades. The share of income going to the middle 50% has declined, while the share of pre-tax income (including capital gains) going to the top 1% earners increased from 10.02% in 1980 to 23.5% in 2007, on the eve of the financial crisis. The proportionate increase for the top 0.1% was even larger; their share increased from 3.41% in 1980 to 12.28% in 2007. To gain a sense of how dramatic this increase income share is, recall that the size of the trade deficit at its peak in 2006 was just under 7% of GDP, which is significantly lower than the increase in the share of income going to the top 1% and the top 0.1% since 1980 (Figure 4.2 (a)). Looked at another way, from 1980 to 2007 real income of the top 0.1% increased by over $6.4 million, while average annual real income increased by $19,000 (Figure 4.2 (b)). The reasons behind the increase in income inequality lie beyond the scope of this book. What concerns this inquiry is how the increased concentration of income may have affected aggregate demand.

The shift in income toward the top raises a vital question as to whether those people "under-consume" their lifetime earnings, or if their consumption follows the PIH.[29] Intuitively, it might seem that people who earn such high incomes would have a tendency to fulfill the common human desire to provide support for their offspring by bestowing inheritances, in which event they must by definition spend less than the income earned over their lifetime. There is, however, an important distinction between people who pass on inheritances they received to the next generation and those who create inheritances out of income earned during their lifetime. The former can spend all of the income earned from the inherited assets and still pass them on to their descendants. That behavior is not Accumulation, because such persons are spending all that they earn. The latter persons, by contrast, must spend less than they earn in order to accumulate wealth they can pass on to their descendants. To the extent top income earners save in order to bestow

DOI: 10.1057/9781137562210.0009

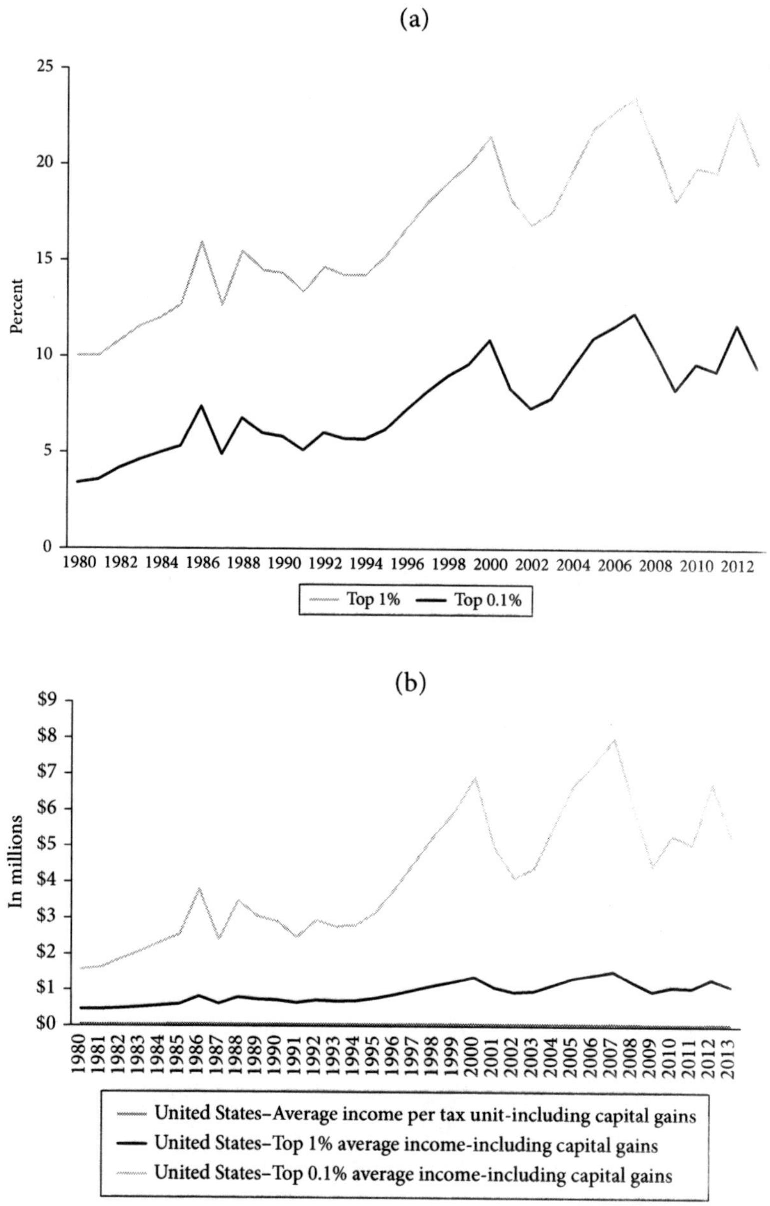

FIGURE 4.2 *The income share and earnings of top 1% and 0.1% of earners in the US (1980–2012)*

Source: Alvaredo, Facundo, Anthony B. Atkinson, Thomas Piketty, and Emmanuel Saez, The World Top Incomes Database, http://topincomes.g-mond.parisschoolofeconomics.eu/, 16/06/2015.

DOI: 10.1057/9781137562210.0009

inheritances on their descendants, they engage in permanent saving. Piketty and Saiz show that most increased wealth in the United States in recent decades has come from wage income, rather than inheritance. This implies that those who leave bequests are likely to have engaged in an increased proportion of Accumulation.

Ideally, one would want to have data on lifetime earnings for a large cross section of the population.[30] Unfortunately, there is no database containing detailed information on the spending habits and earnings of people throughout their lifetimes. The surveys of individual US household earnings and spending collected by the US government[31] do not usually include persons in the top 1% of income distribution, which is the relevant group for this discussion. Moreover, there is considerable controversy over what the extant survey data says about the relationship between consumption and income. The raw data shows that savings increase at an increasing rate as income rises, which is not necessarily inconsistent with the PIH, considering that measured income is for a point in time, not a lifetime. However, the fact that the measured saving increases as income rises does suggest that savings may positively correlate with lifetime earnings, which supports the Accumulation hypotheses. Unfortunately, for this line of reasoning, recent research, which corrects for purported measurement error in the raw data, suggests that consumption rises in line with income, which leaves no room for permanent saving to become larger as income increases.[32]

It is likely that the increase in aggregate measured pre-tax income inequality at a point in time overstates the increase in inequality of lifetime earnings. One reason is that the increase in measured inequality reflects, at least in part, that lifetime earnings have become more peaked as the number of college graduates has increased. The number of people attending college as undergraduates and graduate students has increased markedly in recent decades and it is well documented that increased time in school has the effect of concentrating earnings into fewer years, since students spend more time in school. Therefore, trends in education have generated a disproportionate increase in measured income inequality. Another reason that pre-tax earnings overstate inequality is that it omits the ameliorating effects of progressive taxation and social insurance. The primary beneficiaries of social security, pensions, and Medicare are middle-income persons.

The absence of data tracking the lifetime savings behavior of individuals makes it difficult to gauge the extent to which permanent saving

DOI: 10.1057/9781137562210.0009

among individuals has been increasing. The data that exists pertains to income distribution at a point in time, and does not follow individuals over time. There are, however, two pieces of evidence that lend some support for the thesis that lifetime saving increases at higher levels of income.

One is a study by economists Atif Mian and Amir Sufi that look at spending patterns at the zip code level during and after the housing boom. They find that high-income households adjusted their spending to changes in national income and local housing prices by a lesser amount than lower income households.[33] This lower "marginal propensity to consume" out of changes in income and wealth indicates that high-income households do not readily change their spending when their financial circumstances change. This suggests that high-income individuals may increase saving as their income rises, and thereby spend below their lifetime earnings. Even so, this result should be taken with a grain of salt, since the comparative stability of spending of high-income households to fluctuations in their income and wealth may, or may not, imply is consistency with the PIH. If the affected individuals perceive the increases in income and wealth as permanent, the stability of consumption reflects a higher propensity to save among high earners. However, if they perceive the increase in income as temporary, the stability of consumption may simply reflect that wealthy people have the means to borrow and purchase insurance policies to enable them to smooth their lifetime spending in a manner consistent with the PIH. Since the data do not follow individuals over their lifetime, there is no way to discern which hypothesis is correct. The second is a study by the International Monetary Fund (IMF), which shows an inverse relationship between the income share of the top 20% earners and GDP growth.[34] This is very indirect evidence, but it is consistent with the prediction that an increase in Accumulation slows down GDP growth.

At the end of the day, the lack of data on lifetime earnings and transfers of income through taxation and public goods provision, as well as the inability to discern how individuals view their future earnings prospects, severely limits the degree of confidence with which one can draw conclusions pertaining to lifetime spending behavior from the data on income concentration. Nevertheless, the concentration of income has increased so rapidly, and the amount earned by the top 1% and 0.1% are so huge, that one's intuition (or at least this author's intuition) is that the lifetime earnings of top earners exceeds their lifetime consumption by a

DOI: 10.1057/9781137562210.0009

margin that is vastly greater than the lower income groups from whom they have accrued a transfer of income share.

On that assumption, the shift in income shares away from the middle to the top had the effect of shifting saving from those who tend to follow the PIH to those who are more likely inclined to accumulate and leave inheritances. Under ordinary circumstances, this ought to show up as an increase in the overall household saving rate, given the assumption that top income earners save at a higher rate than middle-income earners. But during the housing boom middle-income mortgage debt—which is a form of negative saving—exploded, which means middle-income dissaving might have fully matched the increase in saving generated at the top.[35] Household saving increased dramatically after the housing boom ended, but it has not (to my knowledge) been possible to discern the extent to which this arose from income concentration, and to what extent it is attributable to the debt overhang created by the collapse in home prices, which barred middle-income earners from borrowing.

In any event, it is important to realize that Accumulation is not determined by the overall savings rate—which actually declined during the housing boom—but by the amount of permanent saving, which likely increased during the housing boom. From this I draw the (very tentative) conclusion that permanent saving among US households increased during the housing boom.

The increased concentration of income as a source of Accumulation

People who spend less than they earn over their lifetime are accumulators. The increase in income share going to top earners raises the prospect that Accumulation has increased. As in the case of mercantilism, Accumulation among the wealthy adds to saving while reducing the return on investment, which creates a savings glut.

3 An interaction between the two sources of Accumulation

The bi-lateral CAD with China caused income concentration to increase through the effect of off-shoring of production, which was motivated by the substitution in favor of lower cost Chinese labor. The effect worked

DOI: 10.1057/9781137562210.0009

through two channels. One was to push down the wages of the unskilled US industrial workers from whom the substitution was made. Economist David Autor and his colleagues find that Chinese manufactured imports displaced middle-income manufacturing employment in the United States in those sectors that competed with China, and the effect was exacerbated by the current account deficit.[36] The other was by increasing the profits of corporations who were able to offshore production. The former reduced the incomes of the middle class, while the latter disproportionately benefitted the wealthy managers who were compensated with share awards and equity owners. Therefore, shrinking the bi-lateral CAD with China should ameliorate Accumulation by reducing income concentration.[37]

4 Market perceptions of Accumulation

An increase in Accumulation implies a reduction in the demand for future goods. As I have explained above, the market reaction can fall between two polar extreme cases. In one case, the Accumulation is recognized by all market participants, in which case it will induce an immediate deflationary contraction. At the other end of the spectrum, Accumulation is not recognized, and investment proceeds and the permanent saving is channeled into investment. This leads to a crisis of over-production at a future time, when customers for the produced goods fail to materialize. Reality is likely to fall in between these two extremes, with some believing, and others not believing, that future demand has been reduced.

5 Accumulation and secular stagnation

The recent rise in Accumulation in the United States began in the late 1990s when Asian nations started to accumulate significant dollar reserves, and income concentration accelerated. For several decades prior to that, the United States had incurred current account deficits, and foreign countries had been accumulating dollar assets. Much has been written about the putative benefits of the "exorbitant privilege" accrued by the United States from issuing the world's reserve currency. It has often been commented that lower interest rates and increased consumption

DOI: 10.1057/9781137562210.0009

subsidized by the rest of the world was "rent" for the use of its currency. In 1971 then US Treasury Secretary John Connelly quipped to a gathering of foreign financial officials: "our dollar, your problem," but that was never the whole story. The chronic current account deficits entailed by the foreign Accumulation of dollars as a reserve asset, reduced aggregate demand in the US economy, while creating a capital flow bonanza. The latter reduced trend growth, while the former increased volatility. This was not a burdensome problem when trade imbalances were relatively small. But it became a major issue when they began to balloon around the turn of the millennium.[38]

By the turn of the century, Accumulation was having a significant effect on the US economy. Labor force participation (as measured by hours of work per household) and the rate of growth of capital per household both began to fall, and median household income growth stagnated (see Figure 4.3).[39] This is the reason Ben Bernanke felt the need to calm deflationary fears while puzzling over the tepid job growth in the recovery from the 2001 recession.[40]

Yet, by mid decade the United States had re-attained full employment. In Aronoff[41] I explain that this occurred because an inflow of foreign capital—which reflected excess offshore saving—pushed down interest rate and triggered a "reach for yield" among financial institutions which expanded the volume of credit. The increased credit was used to finance the housing boom. But, the excess of borrowing and building amidst low and declining productivity growth foredoomed the crisis that followed. The ultimate cause, however, was Accumulation, which was the underlying source of the excess saving, and the cause of the decline in the demand for future goods that eventually brought the boom to its end.

The rise in Accumulation created a tension. It lowered the sustainable level of employment, while at the same time sowing fertile ground for investment and asset price booms. The decline in demand in the US economy caused by the CAD and income concentration tended to reduce aggregate demand and employment, while the increase in saving provided fuel for booms that could temporarily increase spending and employment. Accumulation reduced trend employment over time, while increasing its volatility, as the two opposing forces generated oscillations. Former US Treasury Secretary and economic advisor to President Obama, Lawrence Summers calls the latter predicament "secular stagnation."[42]

DOI: 10.1057/9781137562210.0009

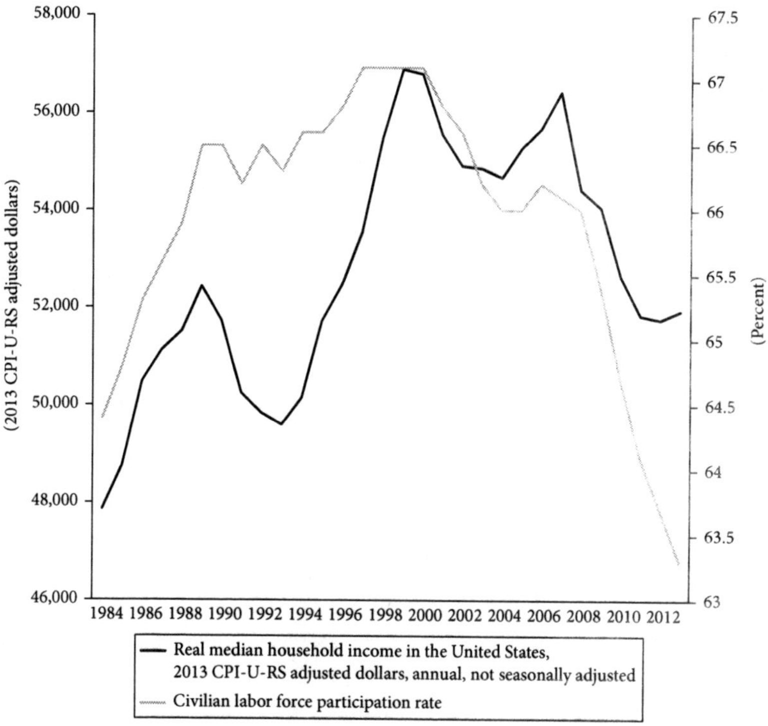

FIGURE 4.3 *US real median household income and labor force participation (1984–2012)*

Source: US Bureau of Labor Statistics.

Prof Summers has placed the issue of secular stagnation at the center of academic and public debate. In so doing, he put forth several possible causes. Investigation of the causes he adumbrated has formed the core research agenda around secular stagnation. Accumulation is related to two of the potential causes he lists—capital flow bonanzas and income concentration. It is worth briefly considering the other potential causes mooted by Prof. Summers.

One idea is that declining population growth will lead to a reduction of investment (and employment related to investment), since it implies there will be fewer customers for future goods. This was a core idea of Alvin Hanson's paper on secular stagnation, from which Prof. Summers

DOI: 10.1057/9781137562210.0009

draws inspiration for his revival of the idea.[43] I argued in chapter 3 that if people spend up to their budget constraints and resources are allocated efficiently, so that markets clear, there will be full employment at any rate of population growth (or decline). Intuitively, a declining population moves through the age brackets, so that there will first be a decline in working age population followed by a decline in retirees. In effect, the reduced number of workers will be investing to support their own consumption in future years. Empirical studies of the relations of population and economic growth support this intuition; they have not uncovered any relationship between population decline and declines in per capita GDP.[44]

Another idea is that the decline in the cost of investment goods (i.e. the materials used in production of final goods) enables all profitable investment prospects to be financed without utilizing all of the available savings. This, it is alleged, creates a dearth of opportunity for profitable investment, and an excess of saving over investment. An excess of saving over investment, as I have explained, reflects a reduction in demand, which will generate deflationary forces. There are three problems with this idea. One is that a decline in investment costs enables a greater volume and variety of goods to be produced, which could spur an increase in both investment and consumption. The second is that (quality adjusted) investment costs have been declining since around 1950 and trend long-run US investment has been stable during that period.[45] The third problem is that a decline in investment opportunities will cause interest rates to decline which, according to the current macroeconomic paradigm, should stimulate consumption, because lower interest rates reduce the amount of future consumption that must be foregone in order to pay for current consumption.[46]

Therefore, I think the capital flow bonanza (which is caused by mercantilism) and income concentration are the most likely causes of secular stagnation, from the group of potential causes adumbrated by Prof. Summers. Insofar as both phenomena are manifestations of Accumulation, it follows that Accumulation is the most likely underlying cause of secular stagnation. It has introduced a chronic weakness into the economy that is occasionally interspersed with unsustainable booms caused by the interaction of low interest rates with institutional structures in the financial sector. There is an alternative explanation, however, that needs to be considered.

DOI: 10.1057/9781137562210.0009

6 Accumulation and the safe asset shortage

Explaining the safe asset shortage theory

A competing theory that purports to explain secular stagnation in the United States during the 2000s is called the "safe asset shortage" theory. To understand the idea, a useful starting place is to note that during the US housing boom of the early 2000s, there was a veritable explosion in the creation of ABS and CDO securities,[47] which were mostly backed by subprime mortgages. These securities were created, to meet the growing demand for safe assets in the early 2000s from institutional investors. The increase in demand for safe assets reflects, in part, the growth of Accumulation—from foreign governments and from wealthy individuals who place their savings in financial institutions. Safe assets are securities that have a negligible risk of default. US government guaranteed debt and AAA-rated securities comprise the bulk of safe assets. Economists Ricardo Cabellaro and Emmanuel Farhi develop a model that purports to show that a safe asset shortage contributed to the stagnant growth and increased volatility of the 2000s.[48] According to Cabellaro and Fathi, an excess demand for safe assets has a similar effect to an excess of desired saving in Keynesian theory. The excess demand for safe assets bids up their price (lowering their yield). If the excess demand remains after the yield on safe assets has reached its lower bound, equilibrium can only be restored when the economy has contracted by an amount sufficient to bring about a reduction in saving large enough to eliminate the excess demand for safe assets. According to their model, that is how a safe asset shortage causes secular stagnation.

An excess demand for safe assets at the lower bound of interest rates is similar to the Keynesian liquidity trap, except in one crucial respect. A Keynesian liquidity trap occurs when aggregate desired saving (at full employment) exceeds aggregate investment. A safe asset shortage, by contrast, pertains to demand and supply of a subset of aggregate saving and investment; that involving the demand for, and supply of, safe assets. There may not be an excess demand for safe assets when the economy is in Keynesian liquidity trap and, conversely aggregate, there can be a safe asset shortage even when aggregate desired saving is equal to investment. Whether a decline in the yield on safe assets will reduce the demand for self assets depends upon the responsiveness of the demand for safe assets to changes in interest rates. If the demand is

DOI: 10.1057/9781137562210.0009

inelastic, it is quite possible that an excess demand (holding constant the supply of safe assets) will cause the interest rate on safe assets to drop to the lower bound without eliminating the excess demand. In fact, one important group of safe asset investors, Southeast Asian and Chinese central banks, continued to pour money into US government guaranteed securities even as their yields plummeted.[49] Cabellaro and Fathi suggest that, in the absence of an increased supply of safe assets, an excess demand for safe assets at the lower bound interest rates will cause a reduction in aggregate demand for final goods and labor, which will create deflationary pressure. During the US housing boom a safe asset shortage was only averted, because two related things occurred. One is that institutional investors shifted some of their portfolios out of safe assets in order to reach for yield, thus reducing the demand for safe assets. The other is that the private sector increased the supply of safe assets by manufacturing pseudo-safe assets out of subprime mortgages, which temporarily abated the safe asset shortage. However, by incentivizing the reach for yield and the creation of private sector safe assets, the safe asset shortage generated volatility. After the financial crisis a safe asset shortage was averted even though the pseudo-safe assets were revealed as unsafe. The supply of government debt increased dramatically and the cash under management of Institutional cash pools receded. Yet, the demand for safe assets—by foreign governments and by Institutional cash pools—looks set to grow and the future supply of US government debt—and the solvency of the US government—is uncertain. So, a safe asset shortage may occur in the near future.

It appears that the safe asset shortage model is intertwined with Accumulation and is able to account for the same patterns of below trend growth and volatility. Both theories posit that a chronic imbalance of saving over profitable investment opportunities—or, in terms of Table 2.1, an excess demand for wealth—is the underlying cause of stagnation and volatility.[50] Yet, it will be shown below that the theory of Accumulation provides a more convincing and comprehensive explanation of the contractionary forces that cause secular stagnation. The difference is that the safe asset shortage theory does not imply a deficiency in demand. In terms of Table 2.1, a safe asset shortage may cause a shifting around of wealth assets without creating a notional excess demand for wealth. Accumulation, by contrast, involves an excess demand for wealth by definition.

DOI: 10.1057/9781137562210.0009

Questioning the dynamics of adjustment to a safe asset shortage

It is possible to question whether a safe asset shortage will set off a process of economic contraction even if a reduction in income is required to restore equilibrium. The fundamental reason for skepticism is that an excess demand for safe assets does not imply any reduction in demand for final goods and labor. This is so for two reasons.

One reason is that the investors in safe assets must place their money somewhere and they are unlikely to hold any significant amount of currency. Therefore, they will have to find other—less safe—securities in which to invest their money. So long as all of their desired saving gets invested in securities, the excess of desired saving intended for safe assets over the supply of safe assets will not cause any drain on final goods demand. This conclusion stands in marked contrast to the dynamics of adjustment to a Keynesian liquidity trap, which involves an excess of desired *aggregate* saving over *aggregate* investment. When total desired saving exceeds the capacity of the economy to provide suitable securities in which to invest, the economy is forced into contraction because excess aggregate saving implies aggregate spending will be below full employment income. Moreover, since every dollar of income is generated by a dollar of spending, a shortfall of spending relative to full employment income will force income to contract. By contrast, a safe asset shortage, unaccompanied by a Keynesian liquidity trap, may push the economy out of equilibrium, but it is not clear how that will affect employment and income. The safe asset shortage model demonstrates that the new equilibrium is at less than full employment, but it says nothing about whether there are forces that will propel the economy toward that new equilibrium.

The second reason an increase in demand for safe assets may not trigger a decline in demand is that the institutions that demand safe assets do not themselves consume and save; rather, they manage assets on behalf of people who do. The existence of an excess of demand for safe assets by those institutions is unlikely to motivate any individual to alter spending habits. For example, nobody's spending pattern will be affected by a gap between the targeted and actual returns earned on US long-term government guaranteed debt by Asia, China, and OPEC. Nor will any individual alter his spending pattern because his Life insurer, defined benefit pension plan or bank experiences a decline in returns on

DOI: 10.1057/9781137562210.0009

investment, at least for so long as they believe that the institutions will make good on their obligations to policyholders and depositors.

Perhaps the underlying reason for the cleavage between excess demand by institutional investors for safe assets, on the one hand, and spending behavior by individuals, on the other hand, is that people view the commitments made to them by institutional investors as a "safe-asset." For so long as the payout commitments by one's insurer, pension plan, money market fund, and bank are not questioned, no change in their investment performance will give reason for any beneficiary to change his plans. Because the safe asset shortage theory does not necessarily cause a deficiency in demand for final goods and labor, I think Accumulation is a more persuasive explanation for the secular stagnation that has plagued the US economy since the turn of the millennium.

In the context of Cabellaro and Farhi's model, it might be possible to differentiate between two types of safe asset shortages, each with different economic effects. One type of safe asset is the payout commitments of institutional investors to their beneficiaries. If the commitments made by those institutions are backed by government, the government is providing beneficiaries with a safe asset, of which there cannot be a shortage for so long as the (often implicit) government guarantee is believed in. A questioning of the government backstop can create a safe asset shortage, however, which can cause individuals to react by reducing their spending, which will cause the economy to contract. The other type of safe asset shortage involves institutional investor demand for safe assets in the marketplace, which can cause asset bubbles by incentivizing a reach for yield or the creation of pseudo-safe assets, such as subprime mortgage backed ABS and CDO. The effects of safe asset shortages can be decomposed as follows: An excess demand for safe assets by policyholders and depositors can cause stagnation, while a safe asset shortage among institutional cash pools and offshore investors can increase volatility.

This conclusion is tempered by two considerations. One is that an increasing portion of the workforce participates in defined contribution pension plans, or otherwise provide for their own retirement. For this group, a shortage of safe investments and/or a steep decline in yields may cause them to reduce spending in order to achieve a targeted level of retirement wealth. The other consideration is that, to the extent companies are required to increase their contributions

DOI: 10.1057/9781137562210.0009

to their pension plans in order to maintain solvency, they will divert into their plans money that otherwise would be available for payouts to shareholders or for investment, which will cause a reduction in spending.

A case for increased government borrowing

A paradox of Accumulation is that accumulators save money and desire to earn a return, but their abstinence ensures that aggregate saving cannot earn a positive return. I believe this inability to generate a return is the fundamental source of the safe asset shortage identified by Caballero and Fathi. Many investors desire to earn a safe return on their savings, but if some savers never plan on spending, there will not be enough inherent return on investment to go round.

Caballero has proposed that the US government issue more debt to satiate the demand for safe assets. On its surface, this may appear to be an idea that will create risk for the US taxpayer and which may ultimately undermine the safety of US government debt. But increasing government debt may be less risky than it appears. Caballero's focus is to have the government manufacture additional safe assets in order to alleviate the safe asset shortage. He places a limit at the government's fiscal capacity, which implicitly assumes all investors in government debt will want to be repaid someday (though new investors might be found to replace them).

The presence of Accumulation enables us to go further in this direction. If the savings really are permanent, and if the interest rate paid on government debt is below the growth rate of the economy, the taxpayer may actually benefit from an increased deficit.[51] If the government transfers the money raised by its debt issuance to non-accumulators, and if the debt is rolled over forever, then it will result in a voluntary transfer of wealth from accumulators to non-accumulators, it will cure the deficiency in demand caused by the Accumulation and it will not crowd out private investment (since the government would be soaking up the excess private savings of accumulators).

Moreover, only government could effectuate this arrangement. Non-accumulators must pay off their debts during their lifetime, in which event the transfer of money from accumulators to non-accumulators (rather than to government) would not increase the lifetime earnings of non-accumulators. In other words, nobody's

DOI: 10.1057/9781137562210.0009

intertemporal budget constraint would be altered, so it cannot boost aggregate demand. But the transfer of money to government, which itself is infinitely lived (or at least longer lived than any individual) never needs to be repaid. Accumulators looking for a safe return will be willing to lend to a creditworthy government, for as long as it remains creditworthy. In turn, the transfer by government of those savings to non-accumulators will effectively enlarge their budget constraints. That is how increased government borrowing could, at least in principle, increase spending, employment, and trend growth. The risk lies in determining the quantity of savings that are truly permanent (or very long lived). It is a very big risk.[52]

7 The dog that didn't bark redux

We are now equipped to answer the question posed at the beginning of Chapter 3: Why did interest rates not rise at the end of the housing boom? What was different this time is that Accumulation grew throughout the boom. The CAD and top income shares soared, which kept interest rates low and created deflationary pressure. Chinese purchases of US government guaranteed debt peaked in 2005–2006, which was the period during which the Fed increased the Fed funds rate.[53] A study by economists Ourda Merrouche and Erland Neir[54] showed that capital flow bonanzas pushed down long-term interest rates in OECD countries in the early 2000s; another study by economists Frank and Veronica Warnock[55] estimated that offshore purchases of treasuries significantly lowered the yield on ten-year treasuries during that time period. The Fed's attempt to stem the tide and lift interest rates was overmatched by these forces. The boom was abetted by a glut of savings, which caused low interest rates and loose credit—something that could trigger a Wicksell/Hayek boom as well—but what ended it was the underlying drain on demand. A dearth of qualified purchasers of the homes produced by the investment undermined the boom.[56]

The dynamics of a boom in an economy suffering from Accumulation can be understood with reference to Table 2.1. At the onset of the boom there was a spontaneous increase in the perceived value of a certain fixed capital asset—homes—which expanded budget constraints and enabled increased expenditure on final goods and homes. Suddenly, people could offer homes as collateral to yield hungry accumulators and

DOI: 10.1057/9781137562210.0009

eliminate the excess supply of final goods and labor by spending the loan proceeds on final goods (or hiring labor to build homes). When home prices eventually collapsed—due to an overexpansion of new homes and a leveraging of existing homes—the value of capital assets declined and budget constraints shrank.[57]

The forces of Accumulation began to loosen the Fed's influence on monetary conditions before the Fed started to raise rates. The expansion in credit and liquidity during the early stages of the housing boom was generated without any notable expansion in monetary policy. The increase in broad money (M2) grew at trend. Credit expanded without any encouragement from the Fed. A study by economist Daniel Thornton provides direct evidence that the relationship between the Fed funds rate and the ten-year treasury yield deteriorated when the CAD began to soar, in the late 1990s. Figure 4.4 shows the results of a regression of

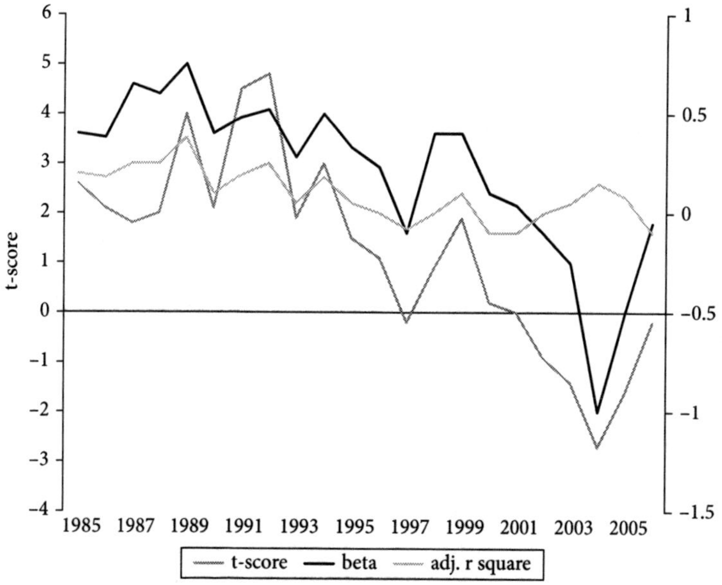

FIGURE 4.4 *Statistical analysis of relation of change in federal funds rate and ten-year treasury yield (1985–2005)*

Source: Thornton, Daniel, L. (2010) *The Unusual Behavior of the Federal Funds Rate and Treasury Yield: A Conundrum or an Instance of Goodhart's Law?* Federal Reserve Bank of Atlanta Mimeo figure 1, p. 55. Data annualized by author.

DOI: 10.1057/9781137562210.0009

changes in the ten-year treasury yield on changes in the Fed funds rate. The regression was estimated using equation (4.2).

$$\Delta\text{Ten-year treasury yield} = \alpha + \Delta\beta \text{ Fed funds rate} + \mu \qquad (4.2)$$

Around 2002, ß, the coefficient on the Fed fund rate, actually became negative, which implies that the ten-year treasury yield declined in response to increases in the Fed funds rate. The T-statistic became larger (in absolute terms), which indicates the accuracy of the measure of ß improved after 2000. But, as Thornton points out, these results are tempered by the fact that R squared, which measures the percentage of variation in the ten-year treasury yield that is explained by variations in the Fed funds rate, was essentially zero from the mid-1990s onward.

Thornton conjectured the deterioration in the relationship between the Fed funds rate and the treasury yield resulted from a Fed policy shift that took place in 1988, long before Greenspan's conundrum. Prior to 1988 the Fed funds rate was set in reaction to the same financial market conditions that affected the ten-year treasury yield, whereas afterward the Fed funds rate was changed less frequently, and sometimes in a direction opposite other market interest rates. I am not going to go into the details of his argument, because it is not relevant to this inquiry, except to note that my proposed explanation is not incompatible with his—it may even be complimentary. The increase in Accumulation is an independent cause of the breakdown in the relationship between the Fed funds rate and the ten-year treasury yield. It explains the intensification of the decoupling that took place in the 2000s.

8 Conclusion

In past booms, the mistake made by investors was to undertake projects assuming that interest rates and input prices would not increase. Eventually, interest rates would spike, input supplies would run low, and their prices rise, at which point it became necessary to abandon some projects. Hayek's fundamental insight that booms originate from an overestimation of potential profits remains valid; it is just that the nature of the misperception changed. In the housing boom, prices and interest rates remained low, and yet the customers

DOI: 10.1057/9781137562210.0009

did not materialize. The misjudgment was a failure to recognize that the nature of saving had changed. The PIH had given way to the age of Accumulation.

Notes

1 Lawrence Summers. Speech at the IMF, November 8, 2013.

2 Malthus, Thomas Robert (1836) *Principles of Political Economy, second edition*, reprinted by August M. Kelly, New York (1964), p. 375.

3 And its existence was to lend credibility to its exchange regime so as to deter the possibility of any future run on its currency in which it would need to be spent.

4 It should also be noted that Southeast Asian countries were forced to manage their exchange rates in order to prevent an appreciation relative to the remnimbi (RMB), since they desired to remain competitive as input suppliers to China's assembly of manufactured goods. This provided an additional reason for them to maintain a dollar exchange rate that resulted in current account surpluses with the United States.

5 For a more detailed explanation of Asian and Chinese currency intervention and reserve policies from the late 1990s through the 2000s, see Aronoff, Daniel (2016) *The Financial Crisis Reconsidered: The Mercantilist Origin of Secular Stagnation and Boom–Bust Cycles*. New York: Palgrave-Macmillan, chapters 1 and 3.

6 Adam Smith, *The Wealth of Nations* Modern Library Edition, Random House Inc., 1994 p. 466.

7 Smith Adam (1776) *The Wealth of Nations*, Modern Library Edition, Random House Inc., 1994, p. 694. The passage quoted in the text, occurs in the context of qualifications to the definition as stated. Smith's concept of mercantilism involved running surpluses in the trade of *final* goods. In order to achieve that end, mercantilists will often restrict exportation of capital goods (or intellectual property) that might aid foreigners in developing competing final goods. Likewise, the mercantilist will promote the importation of capital goods that improve the competitiveness of its exports of final goods. The ultimate goal, however, is the same as stated in the text, to run "an advantageous balance of trade."

8 Ibid., p. 456.

9 Ibid., p. 468.

10 Ibid., p. 715.

11 Many (most?) economists still believe that sustainable full employment can be achieved even if a country imports more than it exports (i.e. runs

DOI: 10.1057/9781137562210.0009

a current account deficit). Greg Mankiw, a prominent contemporary economist, recently wrote: "Politicians and pundits often recoil at imports because they destroy domestic jobs, while they applaud exports because they create jobs. Economists respond that full employment is possible with any pattern of trade." (N. Gregory Mankiw, Economists Actually agree on This: The Wisdom of Free Trade. *New York Times*, April 24, 2015). Some time ago, I published the same sentiment: "... the US has achieved full employment with stable average compensation levels in the face of the huge expansion in the effective worldwide low-cost labor supply, thus proving that a flexible domestic labor market will achieve equilibrium regardless of the external financial balance" (Daniel J. Aronoff, US Has a Stake in keeping China Stable. *Financial Times*, March 17, 2006). I have since come to realize that the full employment achieved during the US housing boom was unstable.

12 The economist reader will note that I am assuming the Marshall–Lerner conditions obtain. The condition is that after the currency depreciation, the sum of changes in export sales and import purchases is positive, measured in terms of the domestic currency. Often, the trade deficit will initially increase after depreciation, as it takes time for the reduction in purchases of imports and the increased sales of exports, to take place. The determinant of whether the Marshall–Lerner condition holds depends upon the elasticity of substitution of imports and exports. Formally, the condition is that the sum of the long-run price elasticities of imports and exports is greater than 1. For example, depreciation against the currency of an oil producer might well result in an increase in the trade deficit, since the price elasticity of the demand for oil is very low. Economists continue to debate whether the Marshall–Lerner condition ultimately holds in most circumstances.

13 In Smith's day, when most currencies were fixed to gold, the country running a surplus would accumulate gold.

14 As before, assuming the Marshall–Lerner conditions obtain.

15 For an analysis of China's trade policies in the 1990s–2000s, see the discussion in chapter 1 of Aronoff, Daniel (2016) *The Financial Crisis Reconsidered: The Mercantilist Origin of Secular Stagnation and Boom–Bust Cycles*. New York: Palgrave-Macmillan.

16 I say "successfully avoided" because deflation might have caused severe economic contraction. For an elaboration on this point, see chapter 9 of Aronoff, Daniel (2016) *The Financial Crisis Reconsidered: The Mercantilist Origin of Secular Stagnation and Boom–Bust Cycles*. New York: Palgrave-Macmillan.

17 Huang, Yasheng (2008) *Capitalism with Chinese Characteristics: Entrepreneurship and the State*. Cambridge: Cambridge University Press, p. 110.

18 For an analysis of China's economic policies in the 1990s, see Huang, Yiping and Kunyu Tao (2011) *Causes of and Remedies for the People's Republic of China's*

DOI: 10.1057/9781137562210.0009

External Imbalances: The Role of Factor Market Distortions. Asian Development Bank Institute WP No. 279, April 2011; Yang, Dennis Tao (2012) Aggregate Savings and External Imbalances in China. *Journal of Economic Perspectives*, 26(4), pp. 125–146.

19 Source World Bank Data, available at http://data.worldbank.org/indicator/NY.GDP.MKTP.KD.ZG?page=1

20 Source WTO April 10, 2013 Press Release Chart 3, available at https://www.wto.org/english/news_e/pres13_e/pr688_e.htm and OECD statistical Extracts database, available at http://stats.oecd.org/Index.aspx?DataSetCode=TISP#

21 Friedman, Milton (1957) *A Theory of the Consumption Function.* Princeton, NJ: Princeton University Press, 2008.

22 See Ando, Albert and Franco Modigliani (1963) The "Life-Cycle" Hypothesis of Saving: Aggregate Implications and Tests. *American Economic Review*, 53(1), pp. 55–84.

23 And today's customers, insofar as they purchase durable assets.

24 A more concise statement is that the demand for labor will shift from the distribution and servicing of current consumption goods to capital goods production. Employment and wages will not necessarily be the same in the two states, but there is no prima facie way to determine how a shift to increased saving will affect the demand for labor in the short run, or over time.

25 The economist reader will recognize this as a restatement of Say's Law; that there will be demand—either as a capital good or a consumption good—for everything that is produced.

26 A central insight of Keynes, however, is precisely that decentralized markets, where savers and investors are separated, sometimes do not "work out" that saving implies future demand. When that happens, according to Keynes, deficient demand causes income to decline until saving has shrunk to a volume that equals investment. That was Keynes's seminal refutation of Say's Law. I shall take a related, but slightly different tack in this chapter. The underlying logic of my point is rooted in Keynes. See Leijonhufvud, Axel (1981) *The Wicksell Connection: Variations on a Theme in Information and Coordination.* New York: Oxford University Press, pp. 131–203, and the discussion in chapter 3.

27 I am also ignoring the effects of constraints that might prevent young people from borrowing. I think I am justified in doing so, since Friedman made a convincing case for the PIH in the 1950s, when the possibilities for borrowing were more restricted than they would become in the decades that followed.

28 For data on the evolution of US incomes over time, see Alvaredo, Facundo, Anthony B. Atkinson, Thomas Piketty, and Emmanuel Saez, The World Top Incomes Database, http://topincomes.g-mond.parisschoolofeconomics.eu/

DOI: 10.1057/9781137562210.0009

29 It is possible that a shift in income shares to top earners who obey the PIH will increase gross saving, since the increase in earnings will cause them to save more in the peak earning years in order to increase consumption after retirement. But these same people will increase borrowing when they are young, so that the increase in saving by peak earners will be matched by increased consumption of non-peak earners leaving aggregate consumption unaffected (assuming a few additional "ceteris paribus" conditions). The text I focus on the changes wrought when the top earners *do not* obey the PIH and leave large inheritances.

30 Friedman, Modigliani, and others who studied savings behavior, deduced aggregate consequences of their hypotheses, and compared it against aggregate data, but they have not ever been able to track behavior of individuals over their lifetimes. The PIH predicted that aggregate consumption would respond very sluggishly—if at all—to changes in aggregate income; a prediction that was at odds with the prevailing Keynesian theory of the consumption function. The aggregate data—much of which had only recently been collected by governments—showed the PIH to be a better predictor of aggregate consumption behavior compared to the Keynesian theory. Consumption did not move in tandem with income. This robust observation was in direct conflict with the Keynesian theory, and was in direct conformance with the PIH. It is much more difficult to differentiate between the PIH and the theory of Accumulation I propose based solely on aggregate economic data. This is so, because there are possible explanations of—for example—secular stagnation—that are compatible with both, or neither one, of the two hypotheses.

31 The US Census Bureau conducts an annual survey of the earnings and spending of a sample of households called the Consumer Expenditure Survey (CEX). The CEX follows households for a maximum of two years (see the CEX website at http://www.bls.gov/cex/ for a description of the CEX). Another survey, the Panel Study of Income Dynamics (PSID), follows middle- and lower income households, and can be found at https://psidonline.isr.umich.edu/

32 See Attanasio, Orazio, Erik Hurst, and Luigi Pistaferri (2012) *The Evolution of Income, Consumption, and Leisure Inequality in The US, 1980–2010*, National Bureau of Economic Research Working Paper No. 17982.

33 See Mian, Atif and Amer Sufi (2014) House of Debt, Chicago University of Chicago Press.

34 *Causes and Consequences of Income Inequality: A Global Perspective* IMF June 2015, available at http://www.imf.org/external/pubs/ft/sdn/2015/sdn1513.pdf.

35 It is also possible that the increase in asset values during the housing boom, which increased household wealth induced people at all income levels to reduce saving.

DOI: 10.1057/9781137562210.0009

36 "Rising imports cause higher unemployment, lower labor force participation, and reduced wages in local labor markets that house import-competing manufacturing industries," see Autor, David, David Dorn, and Gordon H. Hanson (2013) The China Syndrome: Local Labor Market Effects of Import Competition in the United States. *American Economic Review*, 103(6), p. 2121.

37 This conclusion is tempered by the fact that US consumers benefitted from the lower prices paid for Chinese imports. One might argue that gross imports from China reduced US middle-class incomes, but this leaves out possible gains from exports to China. I am not aware of any persuasive evidence bearing on this issue.

38 It was perceived as a problem in the 1980s, when the current account deficit ballooned. At that time Japan and Germany were the principal sources of the current account deficit. The Plaza Accord of 1985, which was prompted by US concerns, led to a coordinated depreciation of the dollar that reduced the current account deficit.

39 See Hall, Robert E. (2014) *Secular Stagnation*. Cambridge, MA: National Bureau of Economic Research.

40 See Bernanke, Ben S. (2002) *Deflation: Making Sure "It" Doesn't Happen Here* Speech before the National Economists Club, available at http://www.federalreserve.gov/BOARDDOCS/Speeches/2002/20021121/default.htm

41 Aronoff, Daniel (2016) *The Financial Crisis Reconsidered: The Mercantilist Origin of Secular Stagnation and Boom–Bust Cycles*. New York: Palgrave-Macmillan.

42 See Lawrence Summer's address at the IMF economic Forum, November 8, 2013. http://larrysummers.com/imf-fourteenth-annual-research-conference-in-honor-of-stanley-fischer/. Paul Krugman stated a version of the secular stagnation thesis two years earlier in his blog. My idea that the current account deficit was a form of Accumulation was inspired, in part, by Krugman's post. But he dismisses the notion that income inequality could be a source of underconsumption based on the fact that household savings had not increased. He assumes that underconsumption—or permanent savings—implies that the overall savings rate must increase. I part company with Krugman on that point, because—as I stated earlier in this chapter—I think it is possible that an increase in permanent saving among top earners can be matched by an increase in borrowing (negative saving) by the middle class, in which event Accumulation would have increased even if aggregate saving had not. I conjecture that this is what occurred during the housing boom. (See Paul Krugman, The Return of Secular Stagnation. *New York Times*, November 8, 2011, available at http://krugman.blogs.nytimes.com/2011/11/08/the-return-of-secular-stagnation/?_r=0).

43 Hansen, Alvin H. (1939) Economic Progress and declining Population Growth. *American Economic Review*, XX!X(1), Part 1, pp. 1–15.

DOI: 10.1057/9781137562210.0009

44 See Eichengreen, Barry (2015) *Secular Stagnation: The Long View* AEA Web. It is certainly possible that if workers and investors are taxed to support retirees, their incentive to work and to invest will be damped. That is a problem the United States will potentially face in the future if it does not reduce Medicare and Social security payout commitments from current levels. But during the 2000s the United States reduced taxes on income and investment earnings, so it was not a concern at the time.

45 Prof. Summers has mooted two other ideas that are not considered in the text. One is that high costs of financial intermediation deter investment. While that does not seem to have been operative during the housing boom, when financial intermediation expanded, Prof. Summers may be correct in supposing that this factor lowers the trend rate of investment, by reducing the net return on investment. The other has to do with the reduced tax incentive to invest at lower interest rates (due to the tax deductibility of interest). Prof. Summers may be right about this factor, but it doesn't address the more fundamental issue of what has caused the decline in interest rates.

46 The macroeconomic paradigm may, of course, be wrong in certain instances. For example, during the financial crisis people reduced their spending as a precaution in response to the fear and uncertainty propagated by the crisis, in spite of negative real riskless interest rates. On the other hand, people nearing retirement might actually increase saving in response to lower interest rates, in order to meet their retirement saving target. There is a heightened possibility that this might have occurred after the financial crisis, which reduced the wealth of aging of baby boomers. This type of reaction would exacerbate the contraction in activity caused by a reduction in profitable investment opportunities.

47 ABS stands for "asset backed securities" and CDO stands for "collateralized debt obligations." They are both types of securities in which the promised payment stream is backed by pledges of cash flow from underlying assets.

48 See Caballero, Ricardo J. and Emmanuel Farhi (2014) On the Role of Safe Asset Shortages in Secular Stagnation, in *Secular Stagnation: Facts, Causes and Cures*. London: CEPR Press, chapter 9, pp. 111–123; Caballero, Ricardo J. and Emmanuel Farhi (2014) *The Safety Trap* NBER Working Paper No. 19927.

49 See the discussion in chapters 3 and 7 of Aronoff, Daniel (2016) *The Financial Crisis Reconsidered: The Mercantilist Origin of Secular Stagnation and Boom–Bust Cycles*. New York: Palgrave-Macmillan.

50 It will be shown that a key distinction is that the safe asset theory posits that an excess of saving cannot be cured by an increase in investment generally, but requires an increase in safe. The safe assets manufactured by the private sector during the housing boom were, it turns out, not safe at all.

51 An interest bill on the debt that is below the growth rate of the economy ensures that non-accumulator borrowers are paying back less than the

DOI: 10.1057/9781137562210.0009

returns generated by the borrowed funds—which ensures they benefit from the transfer. It is possible that non-accumulators could benefit even if the interest bill exceeded the growth rate, but it would require a fully articulated model to work out the conditions under which that result would obtain.

52 The assumption that the market will assume the government can roll over a portion of its debt indefinitely, is, it needs to be emphasized, highly conjectural.

53 For Chinese purchases of Treasuries see US Department of the Treasury, *Report on Foreign Portfolio Holdings of US Securities* available at http://www.treasury.gov/resource-center/data-chart-center/tic/Pages/fpis.aspx.

54 Merrouche, Ouarda and Erland Nier (2010) *What Caused the Global Financial Crisis?-Evidence of the Drivers of Financial Imbalances 1999–2007*, IMF Working Paper 10/265.

55 Warnock, Francis E. and Veronica Cacdac Warnock (2009) International Capital Flows and US Interest Rates. *Journal of international Money and Finance*, 28, pp. 903–919.

56 Mr. Greenspan's failure to understand the source of his conundrum arose from his dismissal of the idea that capital inflows were pushing down long-term interest rates. His contention that "... it is difficult to attribute the long-term interest rate declines of the last nine months to glacially increasing globalization," misses out on the dramatic increase in the capital flow bonanza that was then taking place and its channeling into long-term securities. Mr. Greenspan was led astray by his failure to recognize that the capital flow bonanza was compressing the maturity yield curve. He was not alone in misreading the evidence at the time.

57 For a detailed analysis of the US housing boom and financial crisis, see Aronoff, Daniel (2016) *The Financial Crisis Reconsidered: The Mercantilist Origin of Secular Stagnation and Boom–Bust Cycles*. New York: Palgrave-Macmillan.

DOI: 10.1057/9781137562210.0009

Some Concluding Thoughts

Abstract: *The concept of Accumulation provides a reason (in addition to Keynes's ideas) that aggregate demand should be added to Adam Smith's list of fundamental factors affecting growth and resource utilization in a market economy. Nevertheless, Adam Smith's contentions that the most important factors governing prosperity and growth are the degree to which the rule of law prevails and the amount of investment that is undertaken remain valid. The fact that Accumulation, among other factors, can force an economy out of equilibrium, and eliminate the possibility of an equilibrium, should cause economists to give more consideration to behavior that takes place outside of equilibrium. Doing so may require economists to loosen their adherence to their standard model and embrace the more pluralistic approach to causality advocated by Malthus.*

Keywords: Baran and Sweezy; equilibrium; John Hicks; methodology of economics

Aronoff, Daniel. *A Theory of Accumulation and Secular Stagnation: A Malthusian Approach to Understanding a Contemporary Malaise*. New York: Palgrave Macmillan, 2016. DOI: 10.1057/9781137562210.0010.

 DOI: 10.1057/9781137562210.0010

In the previous chapters, Malthus's idea that excess saving can cause unemployment and stagnation has been explored. I have concluded that his argument is coherent and that it does, in certain circumstances, have relevance to explaining economic events. In this chapter I briefly address some issues to which that discussion gives rise, but which were not included in the main text because they are not central to the matters addressed in this book.

The question of whether aggregate demand is an independent cause of changes in output, employment, and growth is an ongoing subject of debate among economists. Yet, neither Malthus nor new-Keynesians disagree with Adam Smith's contentions that the most important factors governing prosperity and growth are the degree to which the rule of law prevails and the amount of investment that is undertaken. The evidence showing that markets outperform any other arrangement for organizing economic life places Smith's contention beyond the pale of legitimate dispute. A striking example is China. I have described the ill-effects of China's mercantilist policies in these pages, and I have explained that China undertook such policies to alleviate a home-grown problem of excess saving. But the big story about China's economy since the death of Mao, is how the unleashing of market forces, first in agriculture and later in trade, facilitated one of the most dramatic occurrences of economic growth in history.

By comparison to the causal factors identified by Adam Smith, the degree to which aggregate demand affects the economy is small and episodic. It is important to keep that in mind when evaluating policy responses to alleviate problems caused by deficient demand. The rule ought to be that any proposal that would interfere with property rights or dampen the incentive to invest should be avoided if at all possible.

Other than the current malaise faced by the United States, I have not addressed the pervasiveness of Accumulation, around the globe today or in the past. I do not know how widespread a phenomenon it is. I have not undertaken that study. The research program following on the path-breaking work of Carmen Reinhardt and Kenneth Rogoff on the anatomy and causality of financial crises, however, offers some indirect evidence that one cause of Accumulation—mercantilism—appears with considerable frequency and wreaks a good bit of havoc whenever it arises. Their research shows that large capital flows has been a recurring feature of the international economy dating at least from 1800.[1] I argued in Chapter 4 that large net capital inflows are a symptom of

DOI: 10.1057/9781137562210.0010

Accumulation. Insofar as those inflows are caused by deliberate policy on the part of foreign countries, the underlying cause is mercantilism.

There is a non-mainstream school of thought, associated with the work of Paul Baran and Paul Sweezy[2] that, in the tradition of Malthus (they would say Marx) relates Accumulation to the institutional features of the US economy. Their model is sophisticated and compelling, yet I am not persuaded that it is possible to reconcile the record of robust consumption growth in the US economy from the end of World War II to the late 1990s with their explanation that the system has a tendency toward under-consumption. In reading that literature—of which I do not claim comprehensiveness or expertise—it seems there is always some unexpected contingency or other that arises to defer Armageddon.

Finally, I think it should be pointed out that Malthus's attempt to describe behavior that is outside of equilibrium, for which he has been consistently criticized due to the perceived lack of rigor necessarily entailed by such analysis, touches on a vital aspect of economic life to which economists have not given the attention it deserves. I noted in Chapter 2 that economists have avoided dealing with disequilibrium phenomena because their attempts to incorporate it into the theory have so far proved intractable.[3] A perceived solution has been the development of dynamic models of equilibrium, where the equilibrium configuration moves over time, in a stochastically predictable manner. This method has proved fruitful, but it is still limited to descriptions of equilibrium states where all (probabilistic) expectations are met and all plans carried out. There is a need to go beyond that, and in so doing it may require that economists embrace a pluralistic approach to causality, along the lines that Malthus employed. This matter was eloquently addressed by one of the deepest and subtlest economists of all time, the Nobel Laureate Sir John Hicks:

> The more characteristic economic problems are problems of change, of growth and retrogression, and of fluctuation. The extent to which this can be reduced into scientific terms is rather limited; for at every stage in an economic process new things are happening, things that have never happened before... We need a theory that will help us with these problems; but it is impossible to believe that it can ever be a complete theory. It is bound by its nature to be fragmentary. It is commonly called "dynamic" in contrast to "static"; but that is a name which now seems to me to be better avoided. For "dynamics," in its original sense, is a branch of mechanics; and the problems, to which the economic counterpart (if it is a counterpart) refers, are not mechanical. As economics pushes beyond "statics," it becomes less like science, and more like history.[4]

DOI: 10.1057/9781137562210.0010

Notes

1. Reinhardt, Carmen N. and Kenneth S. Rogoff (2009) *This Time Is Different: Eight Centuries of Financial Folly*. Princeton, NJ: Princeton University Press, see figure 10.1, p. 156. Note that the referenced figure is of gross capital flows, while I refer to net capital flows. The details of Reinhardt and Rogoff's analysis make clear that net capital flows—which they call "capital flow bonanza's"—were often quite large and widespread during that period.
2. Baran, Paul A. and Paul M. Sweezy (1966) *Monopoly Capital*. New York: Monthly Review Press.
3. For a notable and highly regarded attempt to incorporate disequilibrium situations into economic theory, see Fisher, Franklin (1983) *Disequilibrium Foundations of Equilibrium Economics*. Cambridge: Cambridge University Press.
4. Hicks, John (1979) *Causality in Economics*. New York: Basic Books, p. xi.

DOI: 10.1057/9781137562210.0010

Name Index

Acemoglu, Daron, 63n15
Aronoff, Daniel, 8n10, 106, 117n5, 118n11, 118n15, 118n16, 121n41, 122n49, 123n57
Attanasio, Orazio, 120n32
Autor, David, 105, 121n36

Baran, Paul, 62, 65n38, 126, 127n2
Becker, Gary S., 58, 65n27, 65n28
Bernanke, Ben S., 85n18, 85n20, 106, 121n40

Caballero, Ricardo, 85–86n21, 109, 113, 122n48
Carlyle, Thomas, 63–64n15
Clower, Robert, 46, 62n6
Connelly, John, 106

Eichengreen, Barry, 121n44

Farhi, Emmanuel, 109, 112, 122n48
Fisher, Irving, 74–76, 78, 85n17, 85n18, 85n20, 86n25
Friedman, Milton, 34, 98–100, 119n21, 119n27, 120n30

Greenspan, Alan, 70, 84n11, 123n56

Hall, Robert E., 121n39
Hansen, Alvin H., 107, 121n43
Hayek, F. A., 69, 84n6, 116
Hicks, John R., 126, 127n5
Hollander, Samuel, 23, 39n40, 42n56, 65n33
Huang, Yasheng, 95, 118n17
Huang, Yiping, 118n18
Hurst, Erik, 120n32

Kates, Steven, 39n40, 65n33
Keynes, John Maynard, 2, 3, 8n1, 8n2, 21, 23, 34, 37n13, 39n40, 43n78, 57, 59–62, 80–82, 84n8, 86n22, 109, 111, 119n26, 120n30, 125
Koo, Richard C., 85n20
Krugman, Paul R., 80, 86n26, 87n27, 121n42
Kunyu, Tao, 118n18

Leijonhufvud, Axel, 46, 62n6, 71, 81, 84n12, 87n28, 119n26

Malthus, Thomas Robert, 2–4, 6, 8n1, 8n5, 16–22, 27–35, 51–52, 53–54, 56–62, 74, 83, 87n29, 89, 98, 125, 126
Mandeville, Bernard, 15, 37n19
Mankiw, N. Gregory, 118n11
Martin, William Machesney, 70
Merrouche, Ouarda, 114, 123n54
Mian, Atif, 103, 120n33
Mill, James, 13, 39n39
Modigliani, Franco, 99, 119n22, 120n30

DOI: 10.1057/9781137562210.0011

Nier, Erland, 114, 123n54

Piketty, Thomas, 100–102, 119n28

Rabin, Matthew, 58, 65n29
Reinhardt, Carmen, 125, 127n1
Ricardo, David, 2–4, 8n1, 8n5, 15–16, 25, 35, 36n5, 37n23, 40n49, 50, 51–52, 53–54, 56–59, 60, 74, 83
Robbins, Lionel, 40n44, 58, 65n26
Rogoff, Kenneth, 125, 127n1

Saiz, Emanuel, 100–102
Say, Jean Baptiste, 3–4, 13, 27, 30–31, 34, 39n39, 39n40, 42n60, 52
Shakespeare, William, 11
Smith, Adam, 2, 4, 8n4, 11–16, 20, 22, 30–31, 36n5, 36n7, 36n8, 36–37nn10–13, 37n18, 37n22, 42–43n69, 68, 83n3, 91–95, 117nn6–7, 118n13, 125
Sowell, Thomas, 37n20, 41n54, 42n55, 42n60
Sraffa, Piero, 2, 8n1, 40n49, 63n7
Sufi, Amir, 103, 120n33
Summers, Lawrence H., 89, 106–108, 117n1, 121n42, 122n45
Sutton, John, 59, 65n31
Sweezy, Paul, 62, 65n38, 126, 127n2

Thornton, Daniel, 115–116

Walras, Leon, 45, 62nn3–4
Warnock, Francis E., 114, 123n55
Warnock, Veronica Cacdac, 123n55
Wicksell, Knut, 69, 84n6
Woodford, Michael, 68, 83n4
Wordsworth, William, 45

Xiaoping, Deng, 95

DOI: 10.1057/9781137562210.0011

Subject Index

Note: 'f' indicates figure, 'n' indicates note, 'nn' indicates note numbers, 't' indicates table.

ABS (asset backed securities), 109, 112, 122n47
Accumulation, 3, 4, 7, 11, 23, 27, 29, 32, 33, 41n52, 58–62, 63n15, 65n38, 68, 86nn23–24, 125–126
  and booms, 77–78
  capital, 11–13, 23, 63n15
  current account deficit as a source of, 91–95, 104
  definition of, 72
  and deflation, 73–77
  growth of, 82, 109
  income concentration and, 104–108
  and increased government borrowing, 113–114
  and Keynesian unemployment, 80–82
  market perceptions of, 105
  of the mercantilist, 89, 91–95, *see also* mercantilism
  and productivity growth, 82, 87n32
  and safe asset shortage theory, 109–113
  and Say's principle, 78–80
  and secular stagnation, 105–108, 112
  of wealth, 5, 17, 36n11, 46, 53, 56, 58, 60, 73, 86n24, 94, 104
accumulators, 4, 5–6, 72, 73, 77, 79–80, 85n14, 86nn22–24, 89, 93, 104, 113–114, 122n51
  see also non-accumulators
agent(s), 5–6, 8n6, 8n9, 11–12, 35, 45–47, 48, 50, 62n4, 63n8, 63n11, 63n14, 65n30, 73, 77, 79, 83, 86n24, 99
aggregate demand, 4, 14–16, 19–20, 23, 25, 35, 37n17, 39n40, 51, 55, 59–61, 89, 100, 106, 110, 114, 125
aggregate excess demand, 5, 48t
aggregate expenditure, 19–20
aggregate income, 19–20, 38n33, 120n30
asset(s), 93, 94, 120n35, 122n47
  capital, 6, 100, 114–115
  dollar, 89, 91, 105
  durable, 98, 119n23
  financial, 45–46, 49
  prices, 75–78, 86n24, 106
  pseudo-safe, 110, 112
  safe, 109–113, 122n50

behavioral economics, 58
boom, *see* boom-bust cycles; US housing boom

DOI: 10.1057/9781137562210.0012

boom-bust cycles, 3, 6, 23–24, 24f, 55–56, 78, 117n5, 118n15, 118n16, 121n41, 122n49, 123n57
borrowers, 6, 69, 72–76, 85n14, 85n19, 85–86n21, 122n51
borrowing, 61, 69, 73, 75, 84n7, 85n14, 89, 104, 106, 113–114, 119n27, 120n29, 121n42
budget constraint, 5–6, 42n66, 45–47, 52, 63n11, 108, 114–115
budget matrix, 45–50, 48t
business cycles, 23, 26, 68–69

capital, *see* capital accumulation; capital assets; capital flow bonanza; capital flows; capital goods; capital investment
capital accumulation, 11–13, 23, 63n15
capital assets, 6, 100, 114–115
capital flow bonanza, 93, 97, 106–107, 108, 114, 123n56, 127n1
capital flows, 125, 127n1
capital goods, 37n21, 51, 52, 55, 65n23, 69, 75, 117n7, 119n24, 119n25
capital investment, 11, 14, 17–18, 26, 39n42, 39n44, 41n52, 50–52, 64n16
capitalists, 6, 17–20, 23–29, 31–33, 35, 38n26, 38n27, 39n42, 39–40n44, 41n52, 42n66, 46, 49, 51–53, 55–57, 61, 64n16, 64n17, 95–96
CDO (collateralized debt obligations), 109, 112, 122n47
China, 6, 7, 78, 89–92, 94–98, 104, 105, 111, 117n4, 118n11, 118n15, 118n18, 121n37, 125
  see also Chinese economic policy; Chinese saving; mercantilist policies of China
Chinese economic policy, 95–98
Chinese saving, 94–99
classes/social classes, 17–18, 18f, 21, 35, 49
consumption, 4, 14, 32, 37n21, 38n28, 38n30, 92, 102–103, 105, 119n25, 120nn29–30
  by capitalists, 28–29, 39n42, 39–40n44, 41n52, 53, 55–56
  current, 36n7, 69, 84n8, 99, 108, 119n24
  future, 36n7, 69, 82, 84n8, 94, 99, 108
  and income, 17–19, 36n11
  and interest rates, 84n8
  and investment, 19, 28, 37n24, 68–69, 73, 77, 99–100
  by landlords, 17, 26, 39n42, 40n45
  and product distribution, 21–22
  and saving, 16–18
  of social classes, 16–19, 18f
  under-, 21, 23, 83n1, 126
  by workers, 16–18, 18f, 25–26, 41nn50–51
contraction, 17, 24, 28, 34, 40n44, 71, 75–77, 79, 80, 85n21, 97–99, 105, 110–111, 118n16, 122n46
current account deficit (CAD), 68, 72, 89–95, 98, 104–106, 114, 115, 118n11, 121n38, 121n42, 123n53
cycles, 3, 6, 8n10, 22–28, 24f, 55–56, 68–69, 78

debt–deflation, 74–75, 76–78, 85n18, 85n20
The Debt Deflation Theory of Great Depressions, 75
deficient demand, 4, 26–27, 31, 33, 41n53, 52, 57, 61–62, 64n17, 73, 78, 79, 94, 110, 112, 113, 119n26, 125
deflation, 40n44, 73–78, 80, 83, 94, 105, 106, 108, 110, 114, 118n16
demand, 3–4, 13, 32
  aggregate, *see* aggregate demand
  deficiency in, *see* deficient demand
  effective, 30, 43n78, 46, 49, 50, 60, 62n4
  for final goods, 16, 20, 23, 25, 26, 33, 49, 50, 52, 53, 57, 63n11, 63n14, 78–79, 112
  insufficient, 15, 16, 57, 78
  labor, 5–6, 25, 28, 57, 64n17, 119n24
  for manufactured goods, 23–24, 31

DOI: 10.1057/9781137562210.0012

demand—*Continued*
notional, 45, 46, 47, 49–52, 62n4, 78–79, 110
planned, 5, 11
and supply, 4, 11, 13, 21, 32, 35, 39n39, 62n4, 84n8
for wealth, 5, 6, 49, 50, 52, 53, 64n19, 78, 79, 98, 110
depression, 3, 6, 15, 71, 74–76
disequilibrium, 30, 35, 59, 126, 127n3
distribution, 17, 18, 21, 40, 56, 96, 100–103, 119n24
"dog that didn't bark," 68, 71, 89, 114–116
dynamics, 29, 37n23, 41n54, 42n55, 42n56, 52–53, 78, 79, 81, 84n10, 111, 114, 126

economic cycles, 22–25, 27–28
economic growth, 3, 4, 11–14, 13f, 78, 86n21, 97, 108, 113, 125
economic theory, 5, 15, 22, 27, 58–59, 63n15, 79, 86n22
effective condition, 20
effective demand, 30, 43n78, 46, 49, 50, 51, 60, 62n4
effective supply, 46
employment, 4, 14, 20–23, 34, 38n28, 41n50, 54f, 55–57, 61, 64n17, 69, 72–74, 78, 87n29, 87n32, 89, 92, 93, 95, 96, 99, 105–107, 111, 114, 119n24, 125
unproductive, 25, 28, 51
see also full employment; full employment equilibrium; unemployment
endowment, 5, 6, 8n6, 47
equilibrium, 5–6, 7, 15, 20, 22, 25, 27, 29, 31, 33, 35, 38n32, 42n62, 52–53, 58–59, 62n3, 62n4, 64n18, 65n30, 68, 70, 77, 80, 81, 86nn24–25, 109, 111, 118n11, 126
see also disequilibrium; full employment equilibrium; general equilibrium
equity, 6, 105

Essay on the Principle of Population, 3
"Euthanasia of the Rentier", 60, 86n22

Fable of the Bees, 15
Fed, 68–70, 114–116
Fed funds rate, 68, 70, 114–116, 115f
final goods, 4–6, 16, 17, 20, 22–30, 32, 33, 37n21, 38n29, 39n39, 45, 46, 49, 50–53, 55–58, 61, 63n9, 63n11, 63n14, 64n19, 78–80, 86n24, 94, 108, 112, 114–115, 117n7
financial assets, 45, 46, 49
financial crisis, 7, 72, 75, 89, 91, 100, 105, 110, 122n46, 123n57, 125
The Financial Crisis Reconsidered, 7, 8n10, 117n5, 118n15, 118n16, 121n41, 122n49, 123n57
frugality, 14–15, 61, 92
full employment, 4–5, 14, 16, 19–20, 22, 25–29, 32, 37n17, 38n32, 40n49, 73–74, 77–83, 93, 95, 106, 108, 109, 111, 117–118n11
equilibrium, *see* full employment equilibrium
wage flexibility and, 53–57, 54f
full employment equilibrium, 11–12, 25, 27, 29, 34, 35, 36n5, 36n10, 53, 79, 80, 82, 83, 86n24

general equilibrium, 42n62, 58, 62n3, 64n18
general glut, 23–24, 29–32, 41n54, 42n55, 45, 50–52, 56–57
goods prices, 24, 52, 73, 75, 78, 85n15
government borrowing, 113–114
Great Depression, 6, 71, 75, 85n17, 85n18, 85n20
Greenspan's conundrum, 68–71, 71f, 83, 84n11, 116, 123n56
growth, 18–20, 22–23, 26–27, 36n6, 51, 55, 63n15, 64n17, 69, 72, 96–98, 103, 108–110
of accumulation, 82, 109
consumption, 18, 126
economic, 3, 4, 11–14, 13f, 78, 86n21, 97, 108, 113, 125

DOI: 10.1057/9781137562210.0012

growth—*Continued*
population, 51, 55, 107–108, 121n43
of output, 12, 13, 13f, 17, 89

housing boom, *see* US housing boom

income, 4, 6, 12, 36n10, 84n8, 91, 96, 119n26
accumulation of, 72
aggregate, 19–20, 38n33, 120n30
borrowers', 74, 75, 76
capitalists', 17, 20, 24–25, 26, 27, 28, 29, 39n39, 49
and consumption, 17–19, 36n11
distribution, 17, 18, 100–103, 101f
and equilibrium, 38n22
inequality, 100, 102, 121n42
labor, 30, 49, 64n17
landlords', 26, 40n45, 40n48, 49
and the non-satiation principle, 33
pre-tax, 100, 102
and spending, 80–81, 86n24, 89, 98, 111
wage, 16–17, 102
workers', 25, 30, 49
see also income concentration
income concentration
and accumulation, 104–108
and permanent saving, 98–104
inflation, 26, 68–70, 76, 83n5, 87n27, 89, 94
Interest and Prices, 68, 83n4, 84n6
interest rates, 16, 26, 34–35, 43n78, 60–61, 68–71, 73, 76–77, 80, 84nn7–9, 96, 105–106, 108–110, 113–114, 116, 122nn45–46, 123n56
International Monetary Fund (IMF), 103, 117n1, 120n34, 121n42, 123n54
inventories, 16, 23, 25, 28, 29, 38n29, 41n52, 47, 57, 63n9
investment, 13, 16–20, 22, 25–28, 36n7, 38n26, 72, 82, 85–86n21, 86n23, 94–96, 105, 114, 119n26, 125
aggregate, 109, 111
boom, 6, 23, 26, 39n42, 69
capital, *see* capital investment
consumption and, 19, 28, 37n24, 69, 73, 77, 99
domestic, 97
over, 26, 70
reduction in, 26, 78, 80, 94, 104, 107, 122n46
return on, 28, 69, 94, 97, 104, 111–112, 113, 122n45
saving and, 20, 34–35, 60–61, 73, 81, 108
"invisible hand", 4, 11, 14

Keynesian/Keynesianism, 16, 34, 62, 80–82, 84n8, 109, 111, 120n30, 125
Keynesian liquidity trap, 34, 80–82, 109, 111
Keynesian unemployment, 80–82

labor, 21–26, 28–33, 38n28, 39n42, 47, 48t, 49–55, 57, 61–62, 63n8, 65n23, 69, 72, 78–79, 92–94, 96, 99, 112, 115
Chinese, 104–105
demand, 5–6, 25, 28, 57, 64n17, 119n24
division of, 11
market, *see* labor market
productivity of, 12
supply, 5–6, 16, 33, 41n50, 54, 62, 64n17, 64n22, 118n11
unemployed, 25, 36n4
unproductive, 17, 23, 37n22, 39n42, 51, 55, 64n21
labor demand curve, 64n17
labor market, 26, 28, 29, 50, 53, 64n20, 81, 84n10, 118n11, 120n36
labor supply curve, 41n50, 64n17, 64n22
laborers, 17, 23, 28, 30, 33, 64n17, 87n29
see also workers
landlords, 17, 18f, 23, 26, 38n26, 39n42, 40n45, 40n48, 49, 51, 63n13, 63n15
law of markets, 23, 32, 39n9, 57, 63n14, 78
lenders, 75–77
liquidity preference, 60–62, 80
liquidity trap, 34, 43n78, 61
see also Keynesian liquidity trap

DOI: 10.1057/9781137562210.0012

luxuries, 16–17, 26, 31–33, 35, 36, 37n24, 38n25, 39n42, 41n50, 43n69, 46, 47, 64n17, 64n22

Malthus, T. R., 2–4, 6, 8n1, 8n5
  debate with Ricardo, *see* Malthus–Ricardo debate
  division of society, 17–18
  elements of approach, 16–22, *see also* Malthus's model
  Keynes' views on, 59–62
  salient differences between Ricardo and, 35
  on wealth of nations, 13–16
  see also *Principles of Political Economy*
Malthus's model
  criticism of, 22–23
  income and consumption for social classes, 17–19, 18f
  income and expenditure assuming constant investment, 19–20, 19f
  movement of output and prices, 23–24, 24f
  paradox of thrift, 21
  pluralistic methodology of, 22
  thematic components of, 23–27, *see also* economic cycles; trend growth/trend
  vs Smith's views on market economy, 16, 20–22
Malthus–Ricardo debate
  on cycle, 27–29
  on money, 33–35
  on trend, 30–33
  outcome of, 57–59
manufactured goods, 12, 16, 21, 23–25, 27, 37n21, 37n22, 54, 117n4
manufacturing, 6, 17, 20, 23–25, 37n21, 38n26, 39n42, 51, 55, 64n21, 65n23, 105, 110
market economy, 4, 11–14, 13f, 22, 36n5, 45, 57, 80, 82, 93, 95
Marshall–Lerner condition, 118n12, 118n14
maximization, 38n30, 58, 65n28
mercantilism, 4, 91–92, 95, 98, 104, 117n7, 125–126
mercantilist country, 92–93, 95
mercantilist policies of China, 7, 89–92, 95–98, 125
mercantilists, 6, 7, 72, 89, 91–95, 117n7, 125
methodology of economics, 7, 22, 125–126
mixed economy, 95–96
money, 3–4, 8n9, 25, 27, 30–31, 33–35, 37n13, 37n24, 38n29, 39–40n44, 41n50, 41n52, 45–47, 48t, 52–53, 58, 60–61, 63n8, 73–74, 76, 85n16, 86n24, 91, 92, 94, 110–115

necessaries, 17–19, 26, 31–32, 41n50, 65n22
non-accumulators, 73, 113–114, 122–123n51
  see also accumulators
non-satiation principle, 5, 8n7, 27, 32–33, 39n41, 46–47, 50–53, 56–58, 61, 63n15, 78–80, 95
notional condition, 11, 20, 38n34
notional demand, 45, 46, 47, 49–52, 62n4, 78–79, 110
notional supply, 45, 50, 51–53, 62n4, 64n17, 79

output, 4, 11–13, 16–17, 19–23, 24f, 25–28, 35, 36n6, 36n10, 37n17, 38n28, 40n44, 41n50, 51, 53, 54f, 55–56, 65n23, 75, 78, 81, 82, 89, 92, 94, 97, 125

paradox of thrift, 21
parsimony, 12, 14–16, 28, 36n7, 36n11
permanent income hypothesis (PIH), 8n8, 73, 98–100, 102–104, 117, 119n27, 120n29, 120n30
permanent saving, 73, 89, 91, 94, 98–104, 105, 121n42
price level, 54, 73, 76–77, 93

DOI: 10.1057/9781137562210.0012

prices, 4–5, 11–13, 16, 28, 33–35, 40n49, 42n62, 45–47, 49–50, 60–61, 64n19, 68, 82–83, 84n8, 85n16, 86nn24–25, 96, 103, 104, 109, 115, 116, 118n12, 121n37
  asset, 75–78, 86n24, 106
  goods, 24, 52–55, 73, 75, 78, 85n15
  market, 30, 36n11, 46, 50
  non-market clearing, 62n4
Principles of Political Economy (Malthus), 13, 16, 22, 36n1, 37n14, 38n31, 38n35, 40n45, 40n47, 43n69, 43n73, 62n2, 72, 83n2, 85n13, 87n29, 117n2
prodigality, 12, 14–15
productivity, 12, 17, 32, 51, 63n15, 82, 87n32, 106
profit, 11–12, 16–18, 20, 23, 24, 25, 26, 28–29, 31–33, 36n11, 38n26, 38n28, 38n29, 39n44, 41n52, 50–52, 55–57, 61, 63n15, 64n16, 74, 80–81, 84n9, 85n16, 93, 96, 99, 105, 116
property rights, 11–12, 125
prosperity, sources of, 11–12, 36n6, 125

recession, 6, 25, 26, 69, 72, 84n9, 84n10, 85n20, 99, 106
Ricardo, D., 2–4, 8n1, 8n5, 15–16, 25, 35, 36n5, 37n23, 40n49, 50, 51–52, 53–54, 56–59, 60, 74, 83
  debate with Malthus, *see* Malthus–Ricardo debate
  salient differences between Malthus and, 35

safe asset shortage, 109–113, 122n48
saving, 6, 20–23, 25–28, 33, 38n27, 69, 77–78, 80–82, 86n21, 108–111, 113–114, 117, 119n24, 119n26, 120n29, 120n30, 120n35, 122n46
  aggregate, 86n23, 109, 111, 113, 121n42
  behavior, 16, 20, 53, 63n13, 72
  by capitalists, 39–40n44, 41n52, 42n66
  by Chinese, 94–99
  consumption and, 16–18
  excess/excess of, 6, 16, 21, 34, 60, 72, 80, 95, 97–98, 106, 108, 111, 122n50, 125
  and growth of output, 13
  household, 97, 104, 121n42
  and investment, 20, 34–35, 60–61, 73, 81, 108
  negative, 104, 121n42
  notional, 60, 61
  permanent, 73, 89, 91, 94, 98–104, 105, 121n42
  planned, 12, 16, 20, 22, 36n10, 60, 81
  rate of, 12–14, 16, 22, 27, 35, 36n10, 97, 99
  see also accumulation
Say's principle, 30, 45–50, 53, 56, 57, 62n6, 78–80, 94
Say's Law, 30, 39n40, 42n60, 119n25, 119n26
secular stagnation, 3, 4, 6, 7, 27, 31, 32, 45, 52, 57, 61, 65n38, 68, 72, 83, 89, 105–110, 112, 120n30, 121n42
Southeast Asia, 89, 91–92, 110, 117n4
State-Owned Enterprises (SOEs), 95–96
supply
  and demand, 4, 11, 13, 21, 32, 35, 39n39, 62n4, 84n8
  excess, 5, 23, 28–30, 31, 49–53, 61, 62, 64n19, 73, 79, 98, 115
  of final goods, 50–53, 61, 64n19, 115
  of goods and labor, 5, 79
  of labor, 5–6, 16, 29, 33, 41n50, 50, 54, 62, 64n17, 64n22, 115, 118n11
  of manufactured goods, 23–24
  of money, 33–35
  notional, 45, 50, 51–53, 62n4, 64n17, 79
  planned, 5, 11

technology, 12, 21, 22, 36n6, 51
ten-year treasury yield, 70, 71f, 115–116, 115f
Tiananmen Square protests, 95
time preference, 12, 34, 36n7

DOI: 10.1057/9781137562210.0012

trade imbalance, 93, 98, 106
trade-off between revenue and profit, 18, 38n28
trend growth/trend, 22, 23, 26–27, 30–33, 72, 89, 106, 110, 114

underconsumption, 56, 99, 121n42
unemployment, 14, 15, 16, 35, 56, 57, 69, 74, 89, 98, 120n36, 125
 see also Keynesian unemployment
US housing boom, 6, 7, 8n10, 26, 68–71, 78, 83, 91, 98, 103–104, 106, 109–110, 114–116, 118n11, 120n35, 121n42, 122n45, 122n50, 123n57

volatility, 7, 83, 89, 106, 109–110, 112

wage flexibility, 28, 29, 35, 40–41n49, 58, 59
 and full employment, 53–57, 54f
wage(s), 4, 5, 16–20, 25–26, 31–32, 38n25, 38n28, 38n30, 40n44, 41nn50–51, 62, 63n15, 64n17, 64n21, 78–80, 84n8, 105, 119n24, 120n36
 flexibility, *see* wage flexibility
 income, 16–17, 102
 real, 54–55, 74, 85n16
 sticky, 73, 74
 and workers, 20, 23, 28, 37n23, 46, 47, 49, 69, 85n16
wealth, 4–6, 11, 17, 45–47, 48t, 64n16, 112, 113
 accumulation of, 5, 17, 36n11, 46, 53, 56, 58, 60, 73, 86n24, 94, 104
 definition of, 8n9
 decline in, 15, 76–77, 86n22, 122n46
 demand for, 5, 6, 49, 50–52, 53, 64n19, 78, 79, 98, 110
 distribution of, 40
 increase of, 14, 21, 25, 91–92, 102, 103, 120n35
 negative, 75
 positive, 5, 63n15
The Wealth of Nations, 11–16, 36n8, 37n11, 37n12, 37n18, 83n3, 91, 117n6, 117n7
Wicksell/Hayek business cycle theory, 26, 69–70, 84nn8–10, 114, 116
workers, 40n48, 51, 81, 92, 96, 105, 108, 121n44
 consumption by, 16–18, 18f, 25–26, 41nn50–51
 indolence of, 33, 41n50, 43n69, 64n17, 64n22
 lay off, 74
 and luxuries, 35, 36n11, 38n25
 unemployed, 16, 25, 56
 and unproductive labor, 37n22, 39n42, 55
 and wages, 20, 23, 28, 37n23, 46, 47, 49, 69, 85n16
 see also laborers

DOI: 10.1057/9781137562210.0012

CPSIA information can be obtained at www.ICGtesting.com
Printed in the USA
LVOW10*2013140116

470676LV00006B/46/P

9 781137 562203